ed Books showing the way

CAL STREET ATLAS

MAIDSTON

BEARSTED · HEADCORN · LENHAM · MARDEN SNODLAND · STAPLEHURST · YALDING

CONTENTS

Page Layout & Road Map 2
3 Miles to 1 Inch

Maidstone Enlarged Centre 3
7 Inches to 1 Mile

Street Maps 4-33
4 Inches to 1 Mile

Index to Streets 34

LEGEND

- Pedestrianized / Restricted Access
- Track
- Built Up Area
- Footpath
- Stream
- River
- Lock Canal
- Railway / Station
- Post Office
- P P+ Car Park / Park & Ride
- C Public Convenience
- Place of Worship
- One-way Street
- i Tourist Information Centre
- 8 8 Adjoining Pages
- Area Depicting Enlarged Centre
- Emergency Services
- Industrial Buildings
- Leisure Buildings
- Education Buildings
- Hotels etc.
- Retail Buildings
- General Buildings
- Woodland
- Orchard
- Recreational / Parkland
- Cemetery

Every effort has been made to verify the accuracy of information in this book but the publishers cannot accept responsibility for expense or loss caused by an error or omission.

Information that will be of assistance to the user of the maps will be welcomed.

e representation on these maps of a road, track or path is no evidence of the existence of a right of way.

Street plans prepared and published by
Red Books (Estate Publications) Ltd, Bridewell House, Tenterden, Kent, TN30 6EP.
The Publishers acknowledge the co-operation of the local authorities of towns represented in this atlas.

006-15/11-04
ISBN 1 84192 381 8

www.redbooks-maps.co.uk

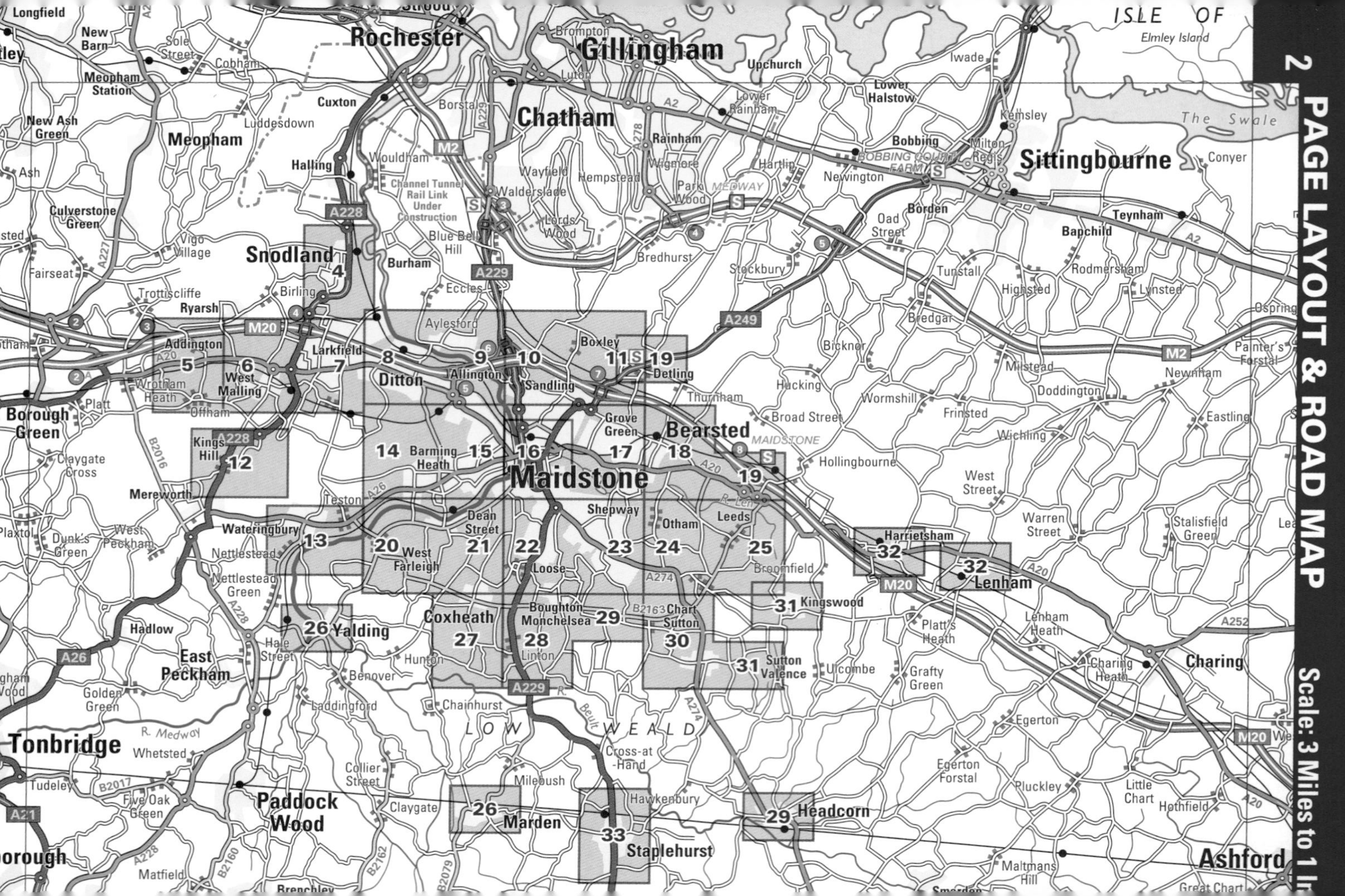

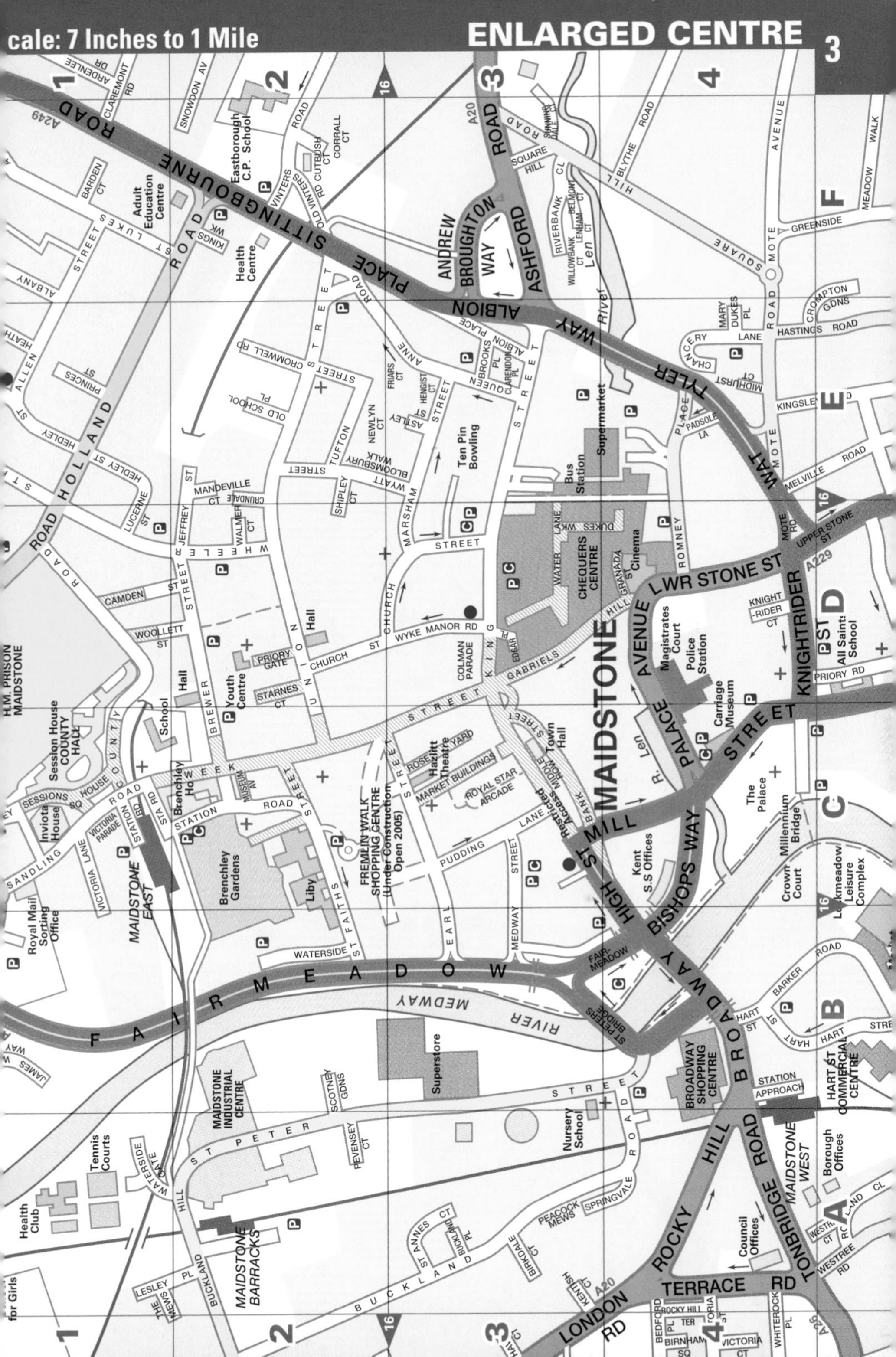
MAIDSTONE
SITTINGBOURNE ROAD
HOLLAND ROAD
FAIRMEADOW
ASHFORD ROAD
ALBION PLACE
TYLER WAY
WAT TYLER WAY
LWR STONE ST
KNIGHTRIDER ST
PALACE AVENUE
MILL ST
HIGH ST
BISHOPS WAY
BROADWAY
ROCKY HILL
TONBRIDGE ROAD
LONDON RD
TERRACE RD
ST PETER STREET
BUCKLAND RD
UNION STREET
CHURCH ST
WEEK STREET
KING STREET
GABRIELS HILL
WYKE MANOR RD
STATION ROAD
CHEQUERS CENTRE
FREMLIN WALK SHOPPING CENTRE (Under Construction Open 2005)
BROADWAY SHOPPING CENTRE
MAIDSTONE INDUSTRIAL CENTRE
MAIDSTONE EAST
MAIDSTONE WEST
MAIDSTONE BARRACKS
H.M. PRISON MAIDSTONE
COUNTY HALL
Session House
Brenchley Gardens
Town Hall
Hazlitt Theatre
Magistrates Court
Police Station
Carriage Museum
The Palace
Millennium Bridge
Crown Court
Lockmeadow Leisure Complex
Kent S.S Offices
Superstore
Supermarket
Bus Station
Cinema
Ten Pin Bowling
Health Centre
Adult Education Centre
Eastborough C.P. School
Youth Centre
Royal Mail Sorting Office
Nursery School
Council Offices
Borough Offices
HART ST COMMERCIAL CENTRE
Tennis Courts
Health Club
All Saints School
River Medway
River Len
A20
A249
A229
A26
16

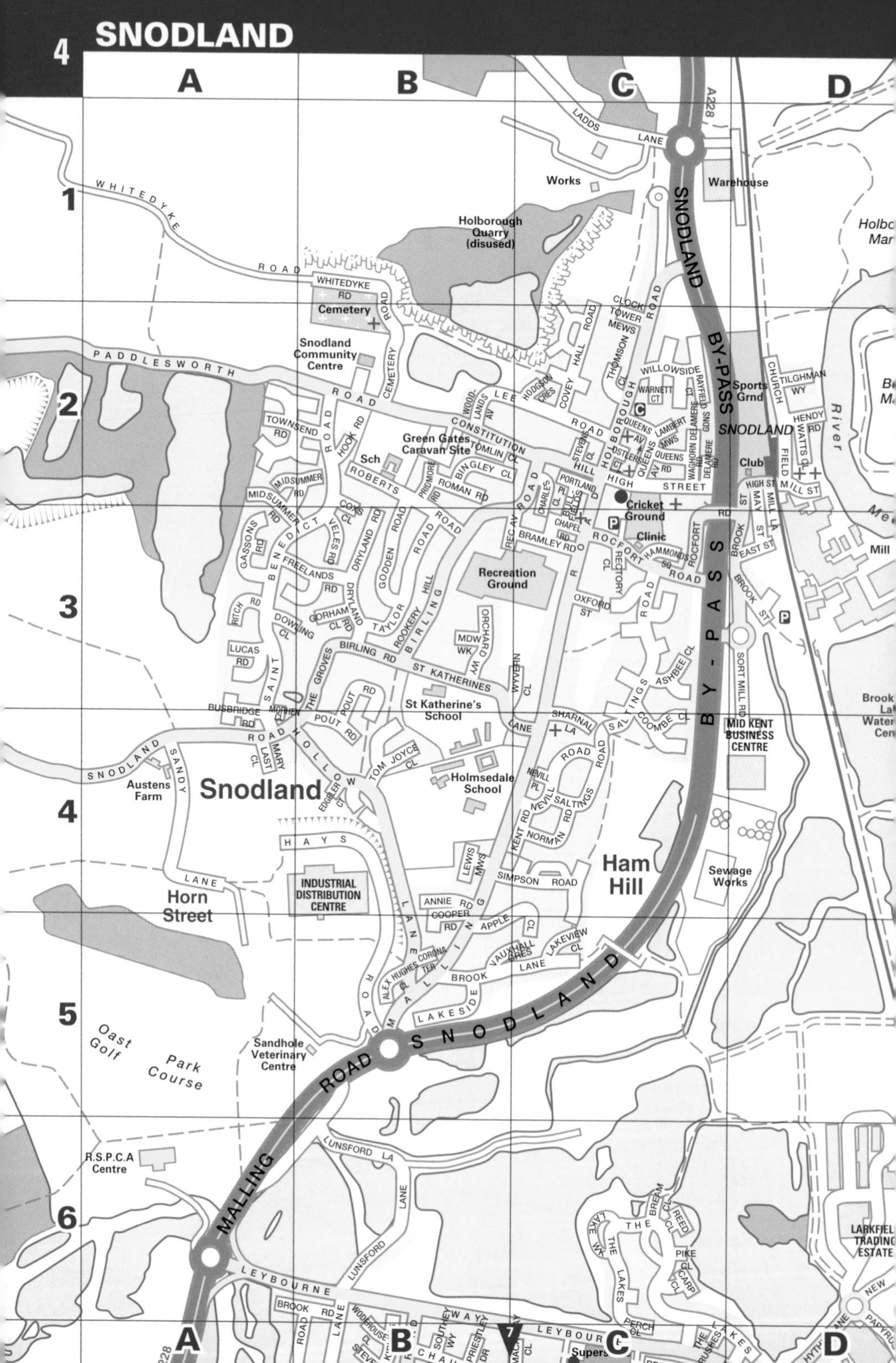
A
B
C
D
1
2
3
4
5
6
WHITEDYKE ROAD
LADDS LANE
A228
Works
Warehouse
Holborough Quarry (disused)
SNODLAND BY-PASS
Cemetery
Snodland Community Centre
PADDLESWORTH ROAD
CEMETERY ROAD
CONSTITUTION
LEE ROAD
Green Gates Caravan Site
Sch
Sports Grnd
SNODLAND
Club
River
Cricket Ground
Clinic
HIGH STREET
Recreation Ground
ROCFORT ROAD
Mill
BIRLING ROAD
ST KATHERINES
St Katherine's School
MID KENT BUSINESS CENTRE
Snodland
Austens Farm
Holmsedale School
HOLLOW LANE
HAYS
INDUSTRIAL DISTRIBUTION CENTRE
Ham Hill
Sewage Works
Horn Street
SIMPSON ROAD
BROOK LANE
SNODLAND
Oast Park Golf Course
Sandhole Veterinary Centre
MALLING ROAD
R.S.P.C.A Centre
LUNSFORD LA
LUNSFORD LANE
LEYBOURNE WAY
THE LAKES
LARKFIELD TRADING ESTATE
NEW
7

A   **B**   **C**   **D**

ADDINGTON LANE

Wealdway

WOODGATE

Ryarsh Wood

ROUGHETTS ROAD

THE

1

TROTTISCLIFFE

EAST STREET NORTH

ROAD

M20

ROUGHE

M20

M20 JUNCTION 3

THE CHESTNUTS

THE GIN

MILL HOUSE LA

ROAD

THE CLOSE

CHURCHFIELD

PLOWENDERS CL

East Street

The Roughetts

2

PARK

ield n

Sports Ground

EAST STREET

6

VINCENTS

LANE

Waterfalls

+

Addington

Plowenders Bridge

WEST MALLING INDUSTRIAL PARK

A20

Addington Park

West Malling Golf Course

ROAD

THE LINKS

ROAD

ROAD

LO

Club House

Sports Field

3

LONDON

LANE

Shaw Hill

Stubbersdown Wood

ALDON

Aldon

ALDON

Moorlands Wood

Church Farm

+

Godwell Farm

4

ALDON LANE

School

6

ESTON

Offham

CHURCH

ROAD

5

Ho Fa

Hook Wood

P

PEPINGSTRAW CL

NORTH MEADOW

Hall

Cricket Grnd

CHURCH ROAD

Nursery

Manor Farm

Waste Management Site

+

ROSE TER

Police Station

ROAD

TEST

Quarry

LANE

The Quintain

HILL

OMP

TOWER

Tower Hill

Offham Wood

Blaise Farm

12

Blaze Wood

A

6

A   **B**   **C**   **D**

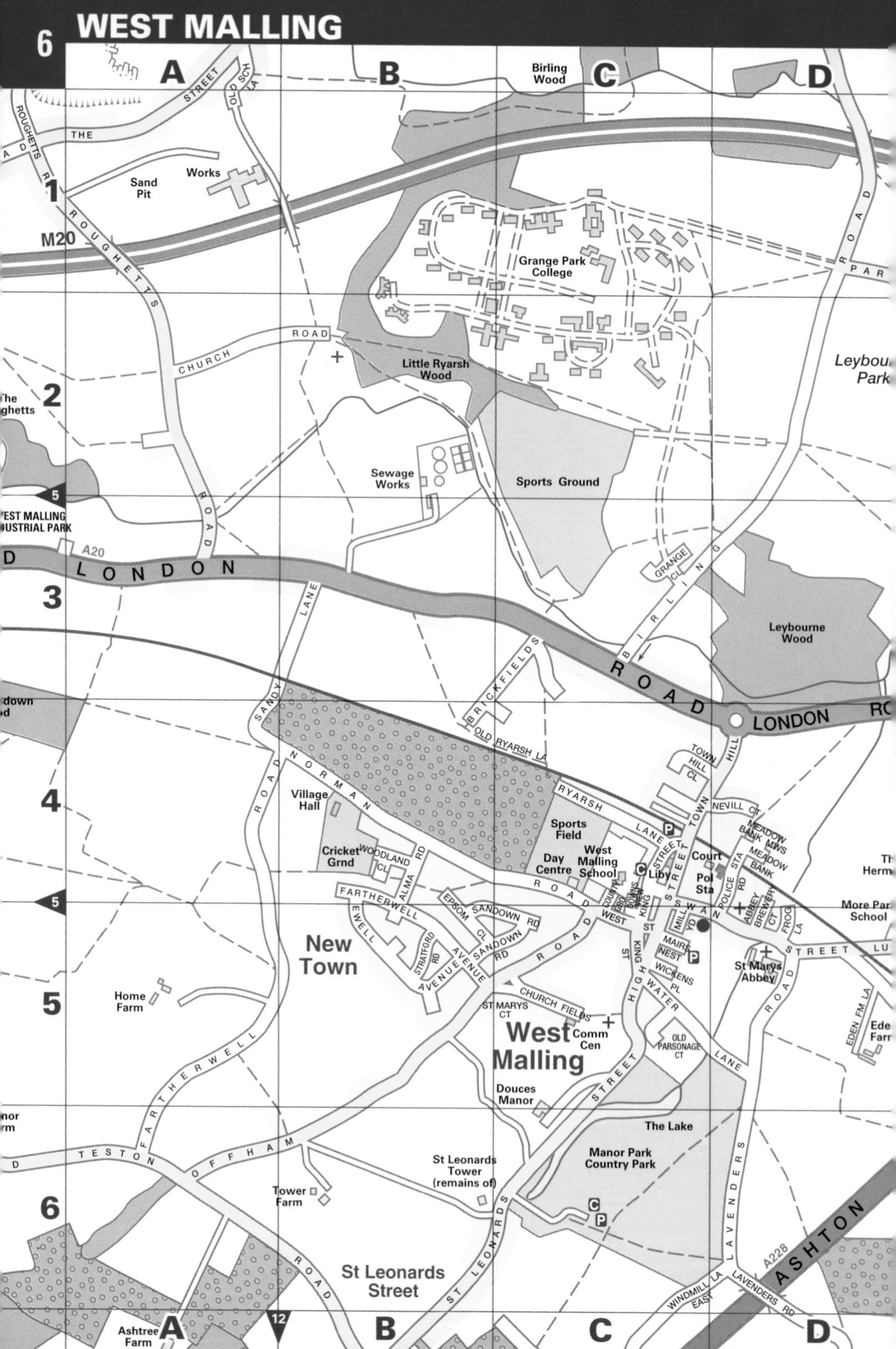

A **B** **C** **D**

Birling Wood

ROUGHETTS RD
STREET
OLD SCH LA
THE

Sand Pit

Works

1

M20

ROUGHETTS

The ghetts

CHURCH ROAD

Grange Park College

Little Ryarsh Wood

2

Leybourne Park

ROAD

PAR

ROAD

West Malling Industrial Park

Sewage Works

Sports Ground

A20

5

D

LONDON

GRANGE CL

BIRLING

3

Leybourne Wood

ROAD

LONDON

LONDON RO

HILL

SANDY ROAD

NORMAN ROAD

LANE

BRICKFIELDS

OLD RYARSH LA

TOWN HILL CL

down d

Village Hall

RYARSH LANE

TOWN HILL

NEVILL CT

4

Cricket Grnd

WOODLAND CL

ALMA RD

Sports Field

West Malling School

Day Centre

Libry

Court

Pol Sta

MEADOW BANK MWS
MEADOW BANK

FARTHERWELL

EWELL

EPSOM CL

SANDOWN RD

ROAD

KING STREET

SWAN STREET

POLICE STA

ABBEY BREWERY CT

FROG LA

More Par School

The Herm

5

New Town

STRATFORD RD

AVENUE

SANDOWN RD

WEST ST

MAIRS NEST

WICKENS PL

St Marys Abbey

Home Farm

ST MARYS CT

CHURCH FIELDS

Comm Cen

HIGH STREET

KING H WATER

OLD PARSONAGE CT

ROAD

STREET

EDEN FM LA

Eden Farr

West Malling

Douces Manor

The Lake

LANE

LAVENDERS

LU

6

nor m

TESTON

OFFHAM

Tower Farm

St Leonards Tower (remains of)

ST LEONARDS

STREET

Manor Park Country Park

P

WINDMILL LA EAST

LAVENDERS RD

ASHTON
A228

Ashtree Farm

A

12

St Leonards Street

B

C

D

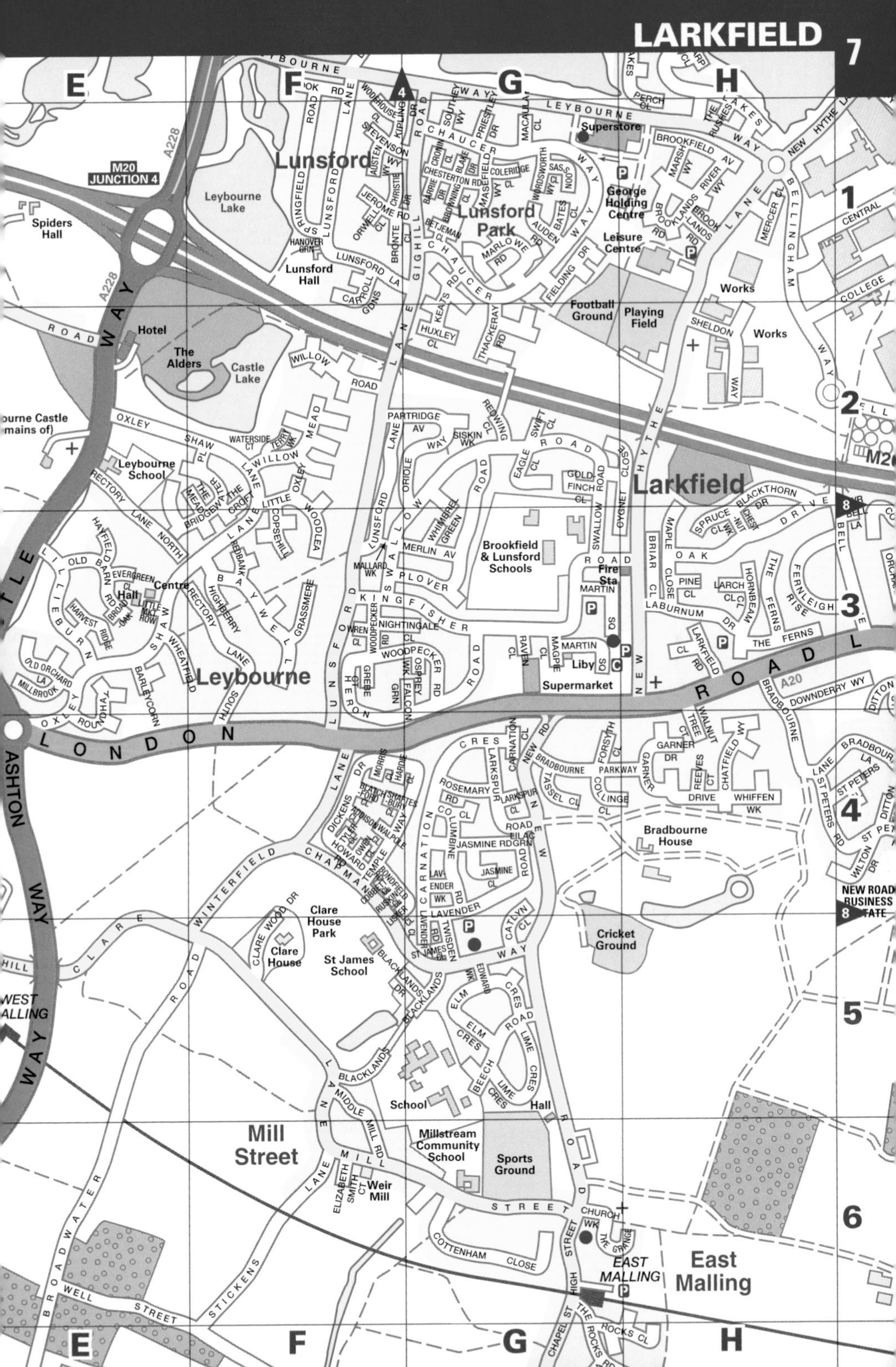

E F G H

Lunsford

Lunsford Park

Larkfield

Leybourne

Mill Street

East Malling

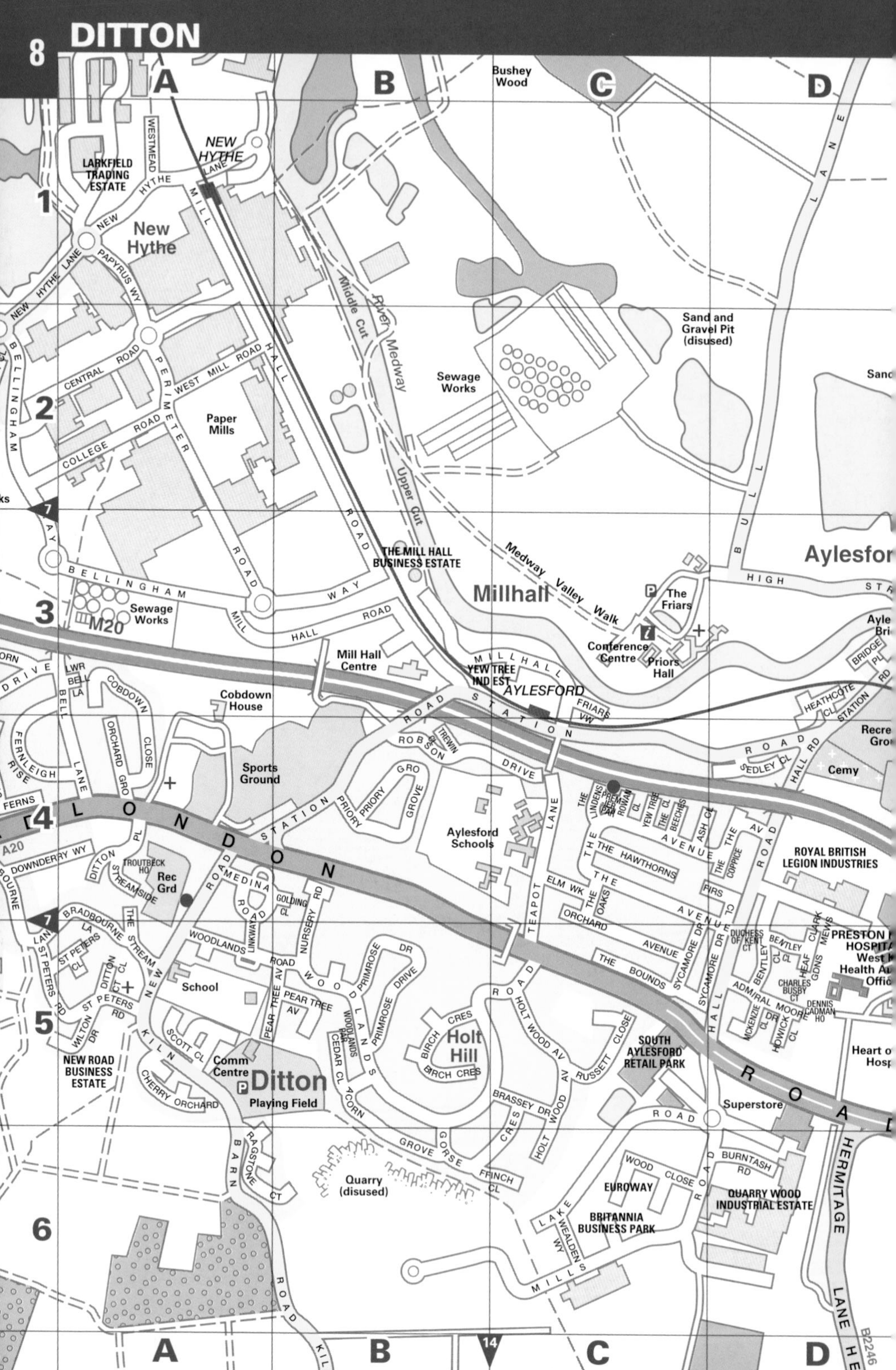
New Hythe
Larkfield Trading Estate
Paper Mills
Sewage Works
Bushey Wood
Sand and Gravel Pit (disused)
Millhall
The Mill Hall Business Estate
Medway Valley Walk
The Friars
Conference Centre
Priors Hall
Aylesford
Mill Hall Centre
Yew Tree Ind Est
Cobdown House
Sports Ground
Aylesford Schools
Royal British Legion Industries
Rec Grd
School
Comm Centre
Ditton
Playing Field
Holt Hill
South Aylesford Retail Park
Superstore
New Road Business Estate
Euroway
Britannia Business Park
Quarry Wood Industrial Estate
Quarry (disused)
Cemy
Preston Hall Hospital
London Road
M20
A20
B2246
Bull Lane
Hermitage Lane
Station Road
Mill Hall Road
Bellingham Way
Medway

E   F   G   H

1

Cowleaze Farm

Little Cossington Farm

Great Cossington

2

Devils Parlour

Marsh Wood

Pratling Street

10
Club House

Peters chool

PLEASANT

UNWIN CL

I POWELL CL

MOUNT RD

BUSH ROW

Comm Centre

Sports Ground

INDUSTRIAL ESTATE

ST MICHAELS

CLOSE

OLD MILL LA

Highway Training Centre

Cobtree Manor Golf Course

3

FORSTAL

DEACON TRADING ESTATE

BEDDOW

WAY

FORSTAL COTTS

SUPER ABBEY ESTATE

Picnic Site

C P

Cobtree Manor Country Park

River Medway

Forstal

Cobtree Wharf

INDUSTRIAL ESTATE

M20

ROAD

4

Sports Ground

COLDHARBOUR

THE OLD OAST BUSINESS CENTRE

Little Preston

Museum of Kent Life

Park & Sail

P

LANE

FORSTAL

Running Round

10

He

The Churchill Centre

EAST PARK RD

M20 JUNCTION 5

COLDHARBOUR LA

20/20 INDUSTRIAL ESTATE

LIPHOOK WAY

LIPHOOK WAY

Lock Wood

CASTLE RD

Tide End Lock

Castle

Alling Mar

5

oyal British gion Village

Allington Quarry

LAVERSTOKE RD

ST LEONARDS RD

ORCHARD BUSINESS CENTRE

ST BARNABAS CL

Allington

AVEN

SPECTRUM WEST

ROAD

Picnic Site

P

Kent Traffic Police HQ

Caravan Site

LONDON RD

ST LAURENCE

Works

Sports Ground

Comm. Centre

P

CAROLINE CRES

BRAUNSTONE

CHARLOCKNE CL

GNEDE CL

BECKENHAM CL

Medway

Cricket Grnd

EGERTON CL

6

LONDON ROAD

A20

BLACKMANSTONE

FORDWICH

HILDENBOROUGH

APPLEDORE CL

HALSTEAD CL

EASTLING

CHERITON

CRESCENT

WYCENT CL

CHENEDE CL

WALK

LULLINGSTONE

STILE

CARLETON

LARKING DR

EYNSFORD DRIVE

STANSTED

CALE

E   F   store L   G   H   Ringles

15
Liby
Allington School

CHATHAM

A
B
C
D
1
2
3
4
5
6
Pilgrims Way
Kent Centenary Walk
Boarley Warren
Tunnel
Channel Tunnel Rail Link
OLD CHATHAM ROAD
A229
PILGRIMS WAY
LIDSING
Boarley Farm
LANE
GREY WETHERS WY
HIGHAM VW
TOLGATE
PILGRIMS VW
BAKERY COTTS
Tyland Barn
Kent Trust for Nature Conservation
TYLAND
SHRUBSOLE DR
Club House
Abbey Gate
SHENLEY GRO
WILLOW INDUSTRIES
Cobtree Roundabout
M20 JUNCTION 6
BOARLEY LANE
Abbey Farm
Boxley Abbey (remains of)
Donkey Shaws
Tunnel
Park Wood
GRANGE
GRANGE LA
FARTHINGS COTTS
YEW TREE COTTS
SANDLING
Running Horse Roundabout
FORSTAL RD
Sandling
Cooke Cottages
M20
Hotel
OLD CHATHAM RD
SANDLING LA
BOARLEY LA
BOARLEY CT
BURLEIGH DR
CUCKOOWOOD AV
SANDBOURNE DR
Cuckoo Wood
Harbourland
Castle
River Medway
Allington Marina
CASTLE DENE
GIBRALTAR LA
RINGLESTONE CRES
TROODOS HILL
COMMAND ROAD
MALDEN DRIVE
THE CRES
WOODCUT
BROOKBANK
BARNEHURST RD
DOWNS CL
VIEW ROAD
ASHBURNHAM RD
Sandling School
BOXLEY
HARBOURLAND CL
BAYMER
ERITH CL
BECKSBOURNE
NEW BARNS RD
DOWNS
DOWNS RD
STOCKTON CL
GODDWIN DR
CLEWSON RISE
NEVILLE CL
CLOSE
STAPLERS CT
Tennis Courts
Clock Tower
Rec Gnd
Medway Valley Walk
PEPPER ALLEY
SHERIDAN CL
ROAD
CHATHAM
Rec Grnd
LUSHINGTON RD
EDNA ROAD
INVICTA PARK BARRACKS
Sports Ground
THE HEDGES
WOODLANDS CL
WOODLAND WY
WORDSWORTH RD
BYRON ROAD
PENENDEN HEATH
DICKENS RD
EGERTON
FINCH CT
Cricket Grnd
CALDER
STANHOPE CL
FAWLEY CL
SPEARHEAD RD
GRAPPLE RISE
PARK LANE
DUNERA DHEKELIA CL
BARBADOS TER
CANADA TER
HONDURAS TER
BANNISTER RD
HILLARY RD
NORTH WY
HEATHFIELD CL
WHEELER ST HEDGES
FARADAY RD
SILCHESTER CT
ROYAL ENGINEERS ROAD
A229
Ringlestone
GAGETOWN TER
GILBERT TER
JAMAICA TER
DRIVE
NORTHDOWN CL
9
9
16

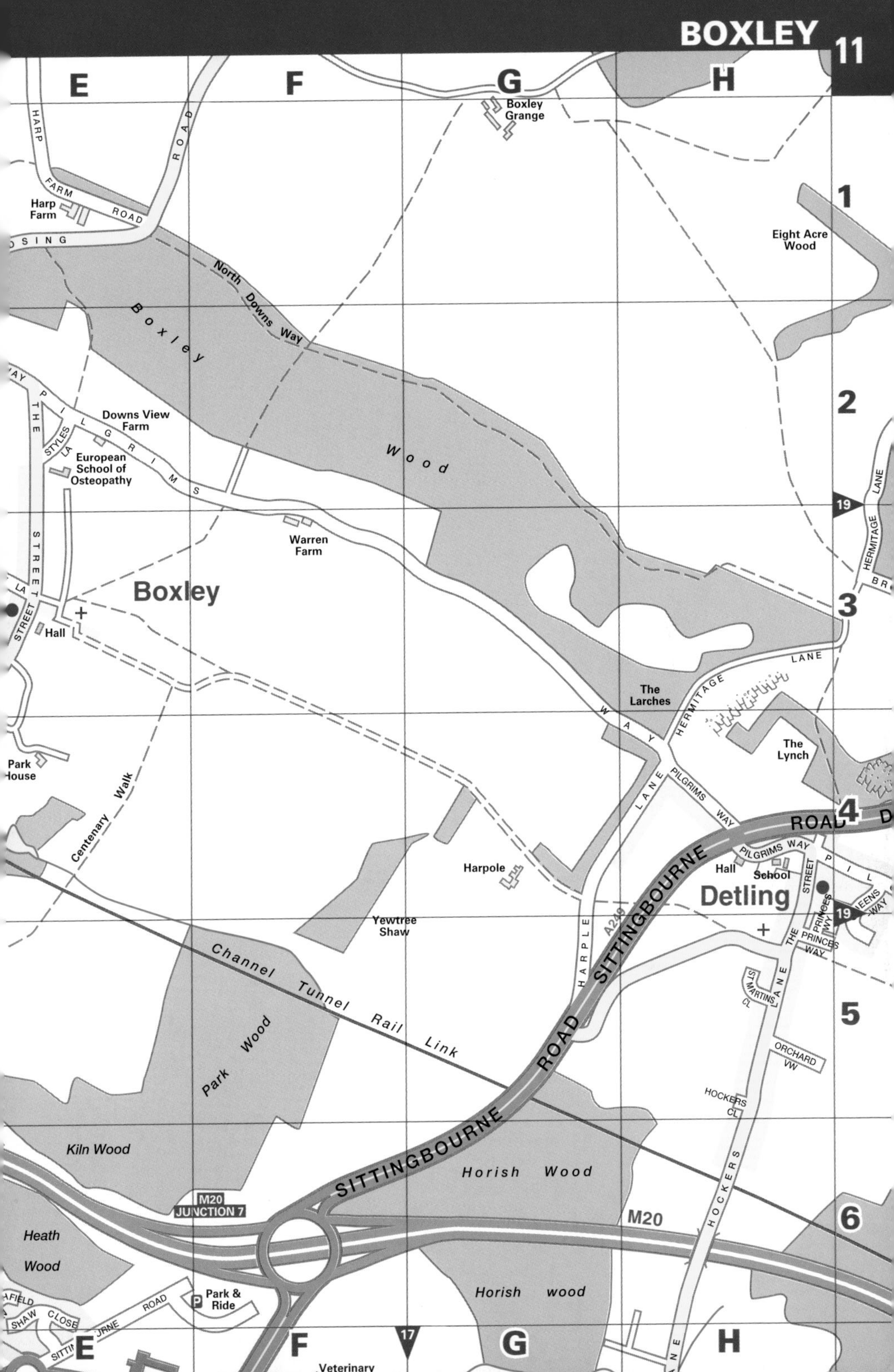

E   F   G   H

1

Eight Acre Wood

Boxley Grange

HARP FARM ROAD

Harp Farm

North Downs Way

Boxley

Downs View Farm

European School of Osteopathy

2

Wood

19

HERMITAGE LANE

Warren Farm

PILGRIMS LANE

THE STYLES

STREET LANE

Boxley

Hall

3

The Larches

HERMITAGE LANE

Park House

Centenary Walk

PILGRIMS WAY

The Lynch

WAY

LANE

PILGRIMS WAY

4

ROAD

Harpole

SITTINGBOURNE ROAD

Hall   School

Detling

19

Yewtree Shaw

Channel Tunnel Rail Link

HARPLE LANE

A249

THE STREET

ST MARTINS CL

QUEENS WAY

THE PRINCES WAY

PRINCES WAY

5

Park Wood

ORCHARD VW

HOCKERS CL

Kiln Wood

HOCKERS LANE

SITTINGBOURNE ROAD

Horish Wood

6

Heath Wood

M20 JUNCTION 7

Park & Ride

M20

Horish wood

FIELD   SHAW   CLOSE   JRNE ROAD   SITTI

E   F   G   H

17

Veterinary

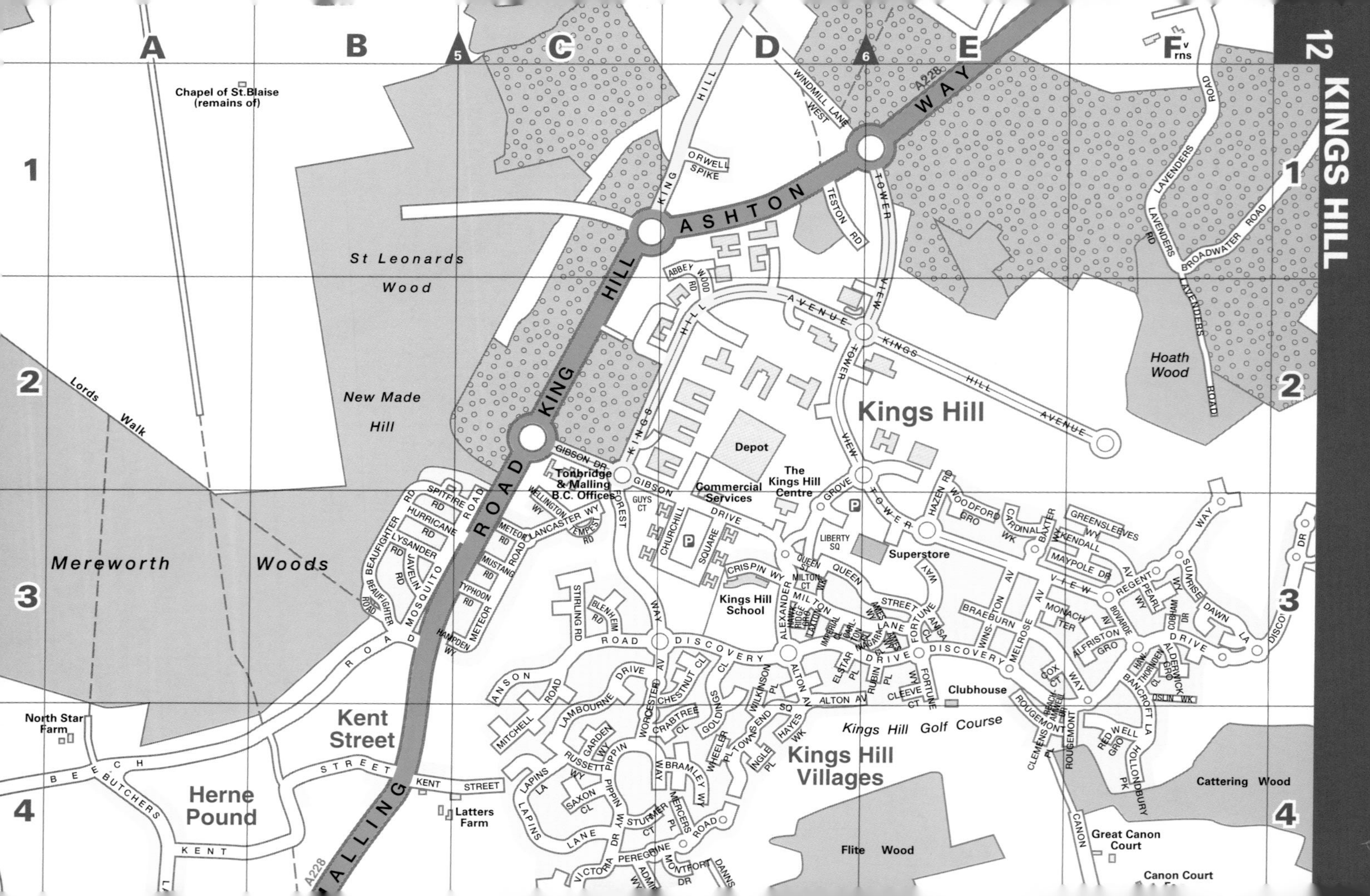

A
B
C
D
E
F
1
2
3
4
5
6
Chapel of St.Blaise (remains of)
St Leonards Wood
New Made Hill
Lords Walk
Mereworth Woods
North Star Farm
Kent Street
Herne Pound
Latters Farm
Kings Hill
Depot
The Kings Hill Centre
Commercial Services
Tonbridge & Malling B.C. Offices
Superstore
Kings Hill School
Clubhouse
Kings Hill Golf Course
Kings Hill Villages
Hoath Wood
Cattering Wood
Flite Wood
Great Canon Court
Canon Court
ASHTON WAY
A228
KING HILL
KING HILL ROAD
ALLING
KINGS HILL AVENUE
TOWER VIEW
WINDMILL LANE WEST
TESTON RD
ORWELL SPIKE
ABBEY WOOD RD
LAVENDERS ROAD
LAVENDERS RD
BROADWATER ROAD
GIBSON DR
GIBSON DRIVE
GUYS CT
FOREST WAY
CHURCHILL SQUARE
LIBERTY SQ
GROVE
CRISPIN WY
QUEEN ST
QUEEN STREET
MILTON CT
MILTON LANE
ALEXANDER GRO
ALTON AV
DISCOVERY ROAD
DISCOVERY DRIVE
FORTUNE WY
ANISA CL
ELSTAR PL
RUBIN PL
CLEEVE CT
HAZEN RD
WOODFORD GRO
CARDINAL WK
BAXTER WY
GREENSLEEVES WY
KENDALL
MAYPOLE DR
BRAEBURN AV
WINSTON AV
MELROSE AV
MONARCH TER
BOVARDE AV
ALFRISTON GRO
REGENT WY
PEARL WY
COBHAM DR
SUNRISE WY
DAWN LA
ALDERWICK GRO
THORNDEN CL
BANCROFT LA
COX CT
ROUGEMONT
CLEMENS PL
RED WELL GRO
HOLLONDBURY PK
CANON
SPITFIRE ROAD
HURRICANE RD
LYSANDER RD
JAVELIN RD
BEAUFIGHTER ROAD
MOSQUITO ROAD
METEOR RD
METEOR ROAD
MUSTANG RD
TYPHOON RD
HAMPDEN WY
WELLINGTON WY
LANCASTER WY
TEMPEST RD
STIRLING RD
BLENHEIM RD
ANSON ROAD
MITCHELL
LAMBOURNE DRIVE
WORCESTER AV
CHESTNUT CL
CRABTREE CL
GOLDINGS
WILKINSON PL
TOWNSEND SQ
HAYES WK
WHEELER PL
INGLE PL
GARDEN WY
RUSSETT WY
PIPPIN WY
BRAMLEY WY
SAXON CL
LAPINS LA
LAPINS LANE
STURMER CT
MERCERS PL
PEREGRINE DR
MONTFORT DR
DANNS
VICTORIA
BEECH
BUTCHERS
KENT STREET
KENT

Teston
Wateringbury
Nettlestead
TONBRIDGE ROAD
MAIDSTONE ROAD
BOW ROAD
A26
B2163
B2015
TESTON LA
Teston Bridge Country Park
Weir
Teston Lock
Tennis Court
Barham Mews
Barham Court Business Centre
WOODLANDS CL
COURTLANDS CL
COURT LANDS
COURTLODGE
CHURCH ST
READERS CT
NESTOR CT
FAIRLAWN CL
MALLING
Tutsham Hall
Marshall's Cottages
HUNT STREET
SMALL PROFITS
Waregraves Wood
River Medway
Sewage Works
Greensted
THE ORPINES
Surgery
Wateringbury Hotel
PELICAN CT
Rec Ground
THE DRIVE
THE BRUCKS
FIELDS LA
COBBS CL
GOODMANS MWS
HANBURY CL
HILLSIDE CT
BOW TER
LENEY RD
RIVERS CL
PHOENIX DR
School
Marinas & Slipway
Bow Bridge
Medway Wharf Marina
Home Farm
Working Mens Club
Hall
ALLINGTON GDNS
GLEBE MDW
Pol Sta
WARDEN MILL CL
WATERSIDE MEWS
ORCHARD CRES
The Retreat Caravan Park
HENRYS CL
GLENLEIGH RD
Bowhill Farm
HUNT ST
KENWARD RD
HILL
Hall
Rec Grnd
LOVE LANE
LODGE CL
Mill Farm
UPPER MILL
MILL LANE
Wateringbury Place
HOUSE GDNS
RED HOUSE
BRYANT CLOSE
BISHOPS CL
King Georges Field
Nettlestead Place
Nettlestead Court Farm
CANON LA
OLD ROAD
Manor Farm
Cemy
Rock Farm
GIBBS HILL
A B C D E F
1 2 3 4

A   **B**   8   **C**   **D**

B2246

HERMITAGE LANE

Laboratories

1

EAST MALLING HORTICULTURAL
RESEARCH CENTRE

Kiln
Barn

KILN BARN ROAD

Knoxes Shaw
Farm

Quarry

Broke
Wood

2

FOUR ACRES
FOUR ACRES DR
THE ROCKS RD
THE ROCKS DR

Kiln Barn
Farm

E A S T E R F I E L D S

Hermitage
Farm

THE ROCKS LANE

SWEETS LANE

3

L'Escargot
Manor House

The Manor
Riding Stables

Fullingpits
Wood

Luckhurst
Farm

*Ditton
Common*

Reservoir

**Barming
Heath**

4

Ce

O a k e n   W o o d

REDE

WOOD

BROOMSHAW RD

Seven
Wents

ROBERTS
ORCHARD
RD

BEECHWOOD
RD

WESLEY
CL

BANKY

MAPLE

POLE

ROAD

NORTH STREET

H E A T H

NORTHFIELD

5

Hall
Place

BELMONT
CL

BEVERLEY DRIVE

MARLBOROUGH
PAR
SOUTHWOOD

N O R T H

APPLE
TREE
CL

Barming
School

BARNED MARYLAND

MATTER
T.RELLY
CL

BELL
FARM
GDNS

BARI

CEDAR DR

MATTERDALE
GDNS

ABINGDON

CT

6

Hall Place
Farm

BULL ORCHARD

SOUTH STREET

RO

GLEB

A   P   **B**   20   + CHURC **C**   LANE   **D**

A26

TONBRIDGE ROAD

PRIORS DEAN
CL

**East
Barming**

CHURCH LANE

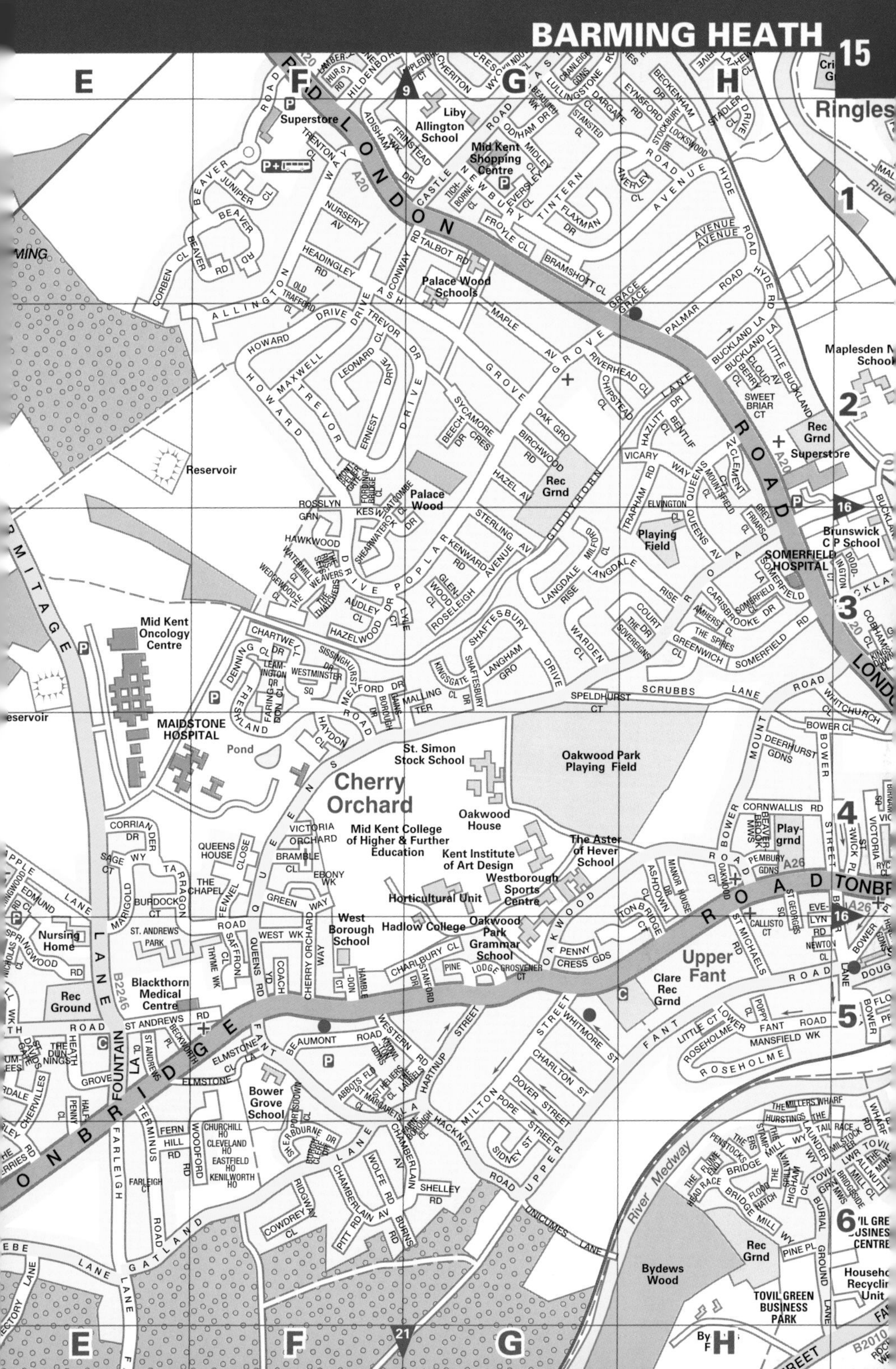
Superstore
Allington School
Mid Kent Shopping Centre
Palace Wood Schools
Reservoir
Palace Wood
Mid Kent Oncology Centre
MAIDSTONE HOSPITAL
Pond
St. Simon Stock School
Cherry Orchard
Mid Kent College of Higher & Further Education
Oakwood House
Oakwood Park Playing Field
Kent Institute of Art Design
The Aster of Hever School
Westborough Sports Centre
Horticultural Unit
Hadlow College
West Borough School
Oakwood Park Grammar School
Upper Fant
Clare Rec Grnd
Nursing Home
Rec Ground
Blackthorn Medical Centre
Bower Grove School
Rec Grnd
Playing Field
SOMERFIELD HOSPITAL
Brunswick C P School
Maplesden N School
Superstore
River Medway
Bydews Wood
TOVIL GREEN BUSINESS PARK
Household Recycling Unit
LONDON ROAD
TONBRIDGE ROAD
A20
A26
B2246
B2010

Ringlestone
Penenden Heath
MAIDSTONE
Tovil
Maplesden Noakes School
Maidstone Grammar School for Girls
North Borough School
St. Pauls School
Russell Hotel
H.M. PRISON MAIDSTONE
County Hall
MAIDSTONE EAST
MAIDSTONE BARRACKS
MAIDSTONE INDUSTRIAL CENTRE
Brenchley Gdns
FREMLIN WK SHOPPING CENTRE (Under Construction)
CHEQUERS CENTRE
BROADWAY SHOPPING CENTRE
MAIDSTONE WEST
HART ST COMMERCIAL CENTRE
Crown Court
Leisure Complex & Mkt Hall
MEDWAY TRADING ESTATE
Kent County Cricket Ground
Maidstone Grammar Sch for Boys
Eastborough C.P. Sch
Invicta Grammar School
FOSTER CLARK ESTATE
St Stephens School
TOVIL GREEN BUSINESS CENTRE
Household Recycling Unit
Postley Commercial Centre
South Borough Training & Development Centre
Playing Field Gymnasium & Health Club
Millenium Ho
Park Way School
Bus Depot
Brunswick C P School
River Medway
FAIRMEADOW
LONDON RD
TONBRIDGE RD
ALBION PL
SITTINGBOURNE RD
ASHFORD RD
UPR STONE ST
LOOSE RD
HAYLE RD
HOLLAND RD
BOXLEY RD
ENGINEERS RD
ROYAL ENGINEERS RD
HIGH ST
KING STREET
MILL ST
COLLEGE RD
PALACE AV
TOVIL HILL
FARLEIGH HILL
MOTE AVENUE
A229
A20
A26
A249
B2012
B2010
15
10
22

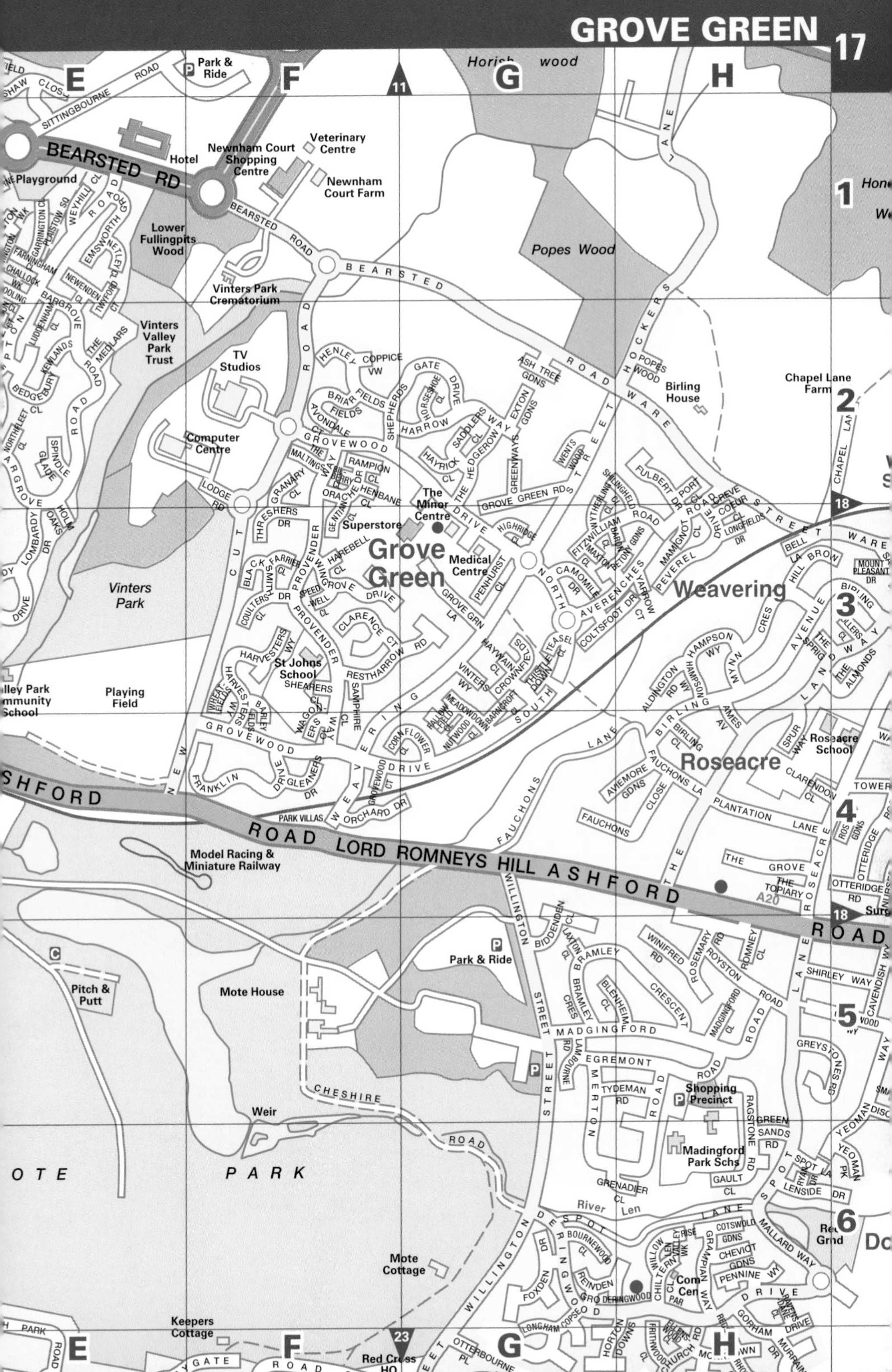

E F 11 G H

Horish wood

Park & Ride

Sittingbourne Road

BEARSTED RD

Hotel
Newnham Court Shopping Centre
Veterinary Centre
Newnham Court Farm

Playground

Bearsted Road

BEARSTED

Lower Fullingpits Wood

Popes Wood

1

Vinters Park Crematorium

Vinters Valley Park Trust

TV Studios

Henley
Coppice
VW

Gate

Ash Tree Gdns

Popes Wood

Birling House

Chapel Lane Farm

2

Computer Centre

Grovewood

Briar Fields
Avondale
Shepherds
Horseshoe
Harrow

Saddlers Way
Exton
Greenways
Hayrick Cl

Wents

Fulbert Rd

Lodge Rd

The Maltings
Granary
Berry
Oracle
Henbane Cl
Rampion Cl

The Minor Centre

Grove Green Rd

Springhill

Port

18

Grove
Green

Threshers Dr
Black Farriers
Coulters
Speedwell
Provender
Harebell
Winslow
Horse

Superstore

Medical Centre

Highrise
Penhurst

Fitzwilliam
William Rd

Camomile

Pevrel

Bell

Mount Pleasant Dr

Vinters Park

Clarence Ct
Provender
Clarence Ct
Restharrow Rd

Grove Grn La
Grove Green
North
Haymain

Averenches
Coltsfoot Dr
Teasel
Harrow

Weavering

Cres

The Spring

The Almonds

3

St Johns School
Harvesters
Barley
Shearers
Samphire

Vinters Way
Crownfld
Cornfield
Meadowsw

South

Hampson Wy
Hampson
Aldington Rd
Birling La
Ames
Birling

Spur Wy

Roseacre School

Playing Field

Grovewood
Franklin
Gleaners Dr

Cornflower
Ravenwood
Orchard Dr

Fauchons La

Avemore Gdns
Close

Fauchons

Roseacre

Clarendon Cl

Plantation Lane

Tower

4

Park Villas

Weavering
Drive

ASHFORD

Model Racing & Miniature Railway

ROAD LORD ROMNEYS HILL ASHFORD

The

The Grove

Otteridge Rd

18

ROAD

Pitch & Putt

Mote House

Park & Ride

Madingford
Street
Biddenden
Laxton
Bramley
Blenheim
Cres
Crescent

Winifred Rd
Rosemary Rd
Royston

Romney Cl

Shirley Way

Cavendish La

Greystones

5

Egremont
Merton
Tydeman Rd

Shopping Precinct

Madingford Park Schs

Green Sands

Spot La
Lenside Dr

Yeoman Pk

Cheshire Road

Grenadier
Gault Cl

6

Weir

MOTE PARK

River Len

Mallard Way

Red Gnd

Do

Mote Cottage

Willington Street
Bournewood Dr
Foxden
Deringwood Drive
Chill Willow
Chiltern
Copsed
Horton Downs
Church Rd

Cotswold Gdns
Cheviot Gdns
Pennine Wy

Com Cen

Gorham Drive

Keepers Cottage

23

Red Cross HQ

E F G H

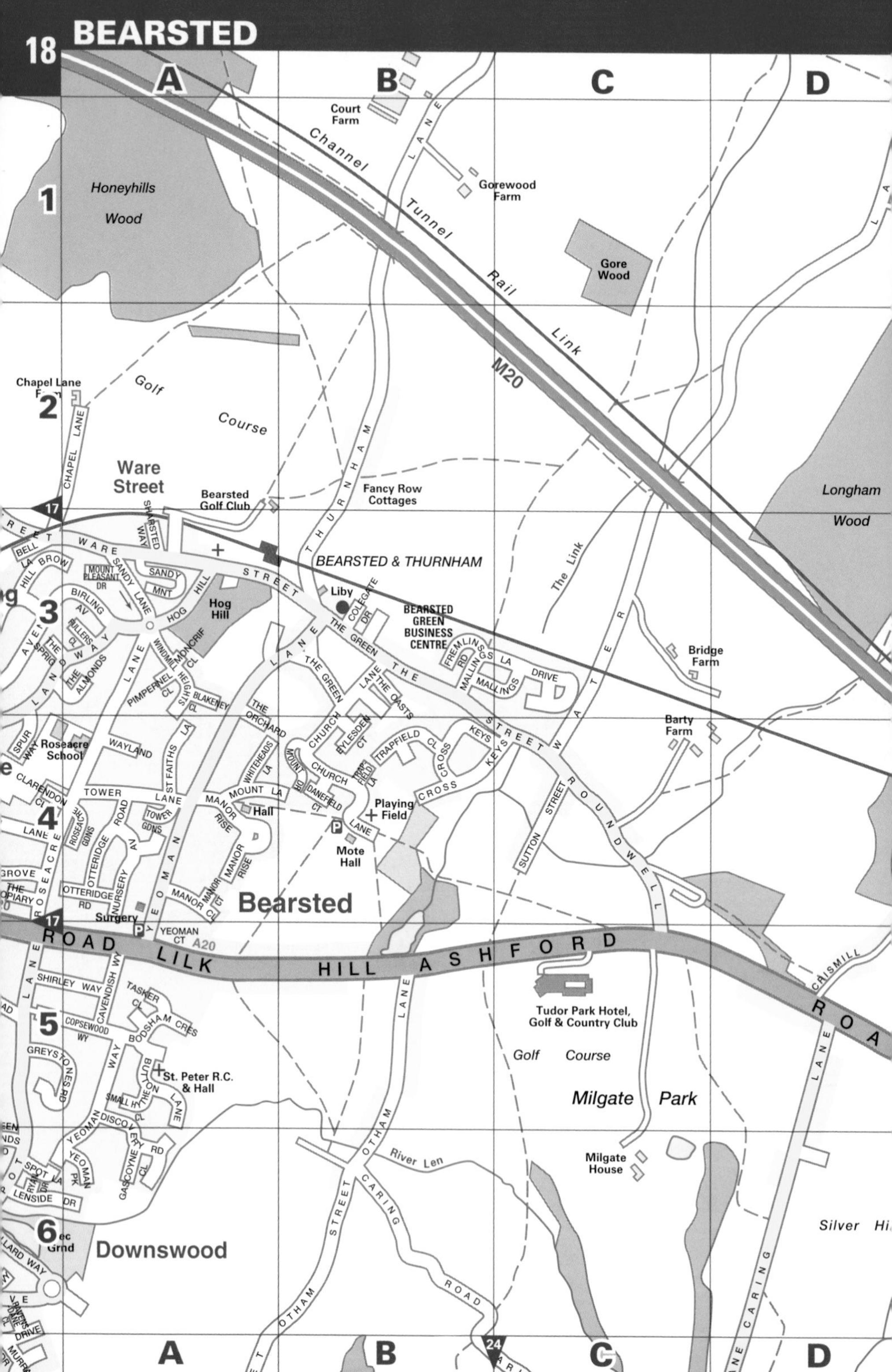

A Honeyhills Wood

B Court Farm

Gorewood Farm

Gore Wood

C

D

Channel Tunnel Rail Link

M20

1

2 Chapel Lane

Golf Course

Ware Street

Bearsted Golf Club

Fancy Row Cottages

Longham Wood

BEARSTED & THURNHAM

Libry

BEARSTED GREEN BUSINESS CENTRE

Bridge Farm

3 Birling

Hog Hill

The Green

Barty Farm

Roseacre School

Wayland

The Orchard

Church Lane

Trapfield Cl

Keys Cross

4 Clarendon Ct

Tower Road

Manor Rise

Hall

Playing Field

Mote Hall

Sutton Street

Bearsted

Surgery

17 ROAD LILK HILL ASHFORD ROAD

Yeoman Ct A20

Crismill

5 Shirley Way

Copsewood Wy

St. Peter R.C. & Hall

Tudor Park Hotel, Golf & Country Club

Golf Course

Milgate Park

Milgate House

6 Downswood

River Len

Silver Hi

A B **24** C D

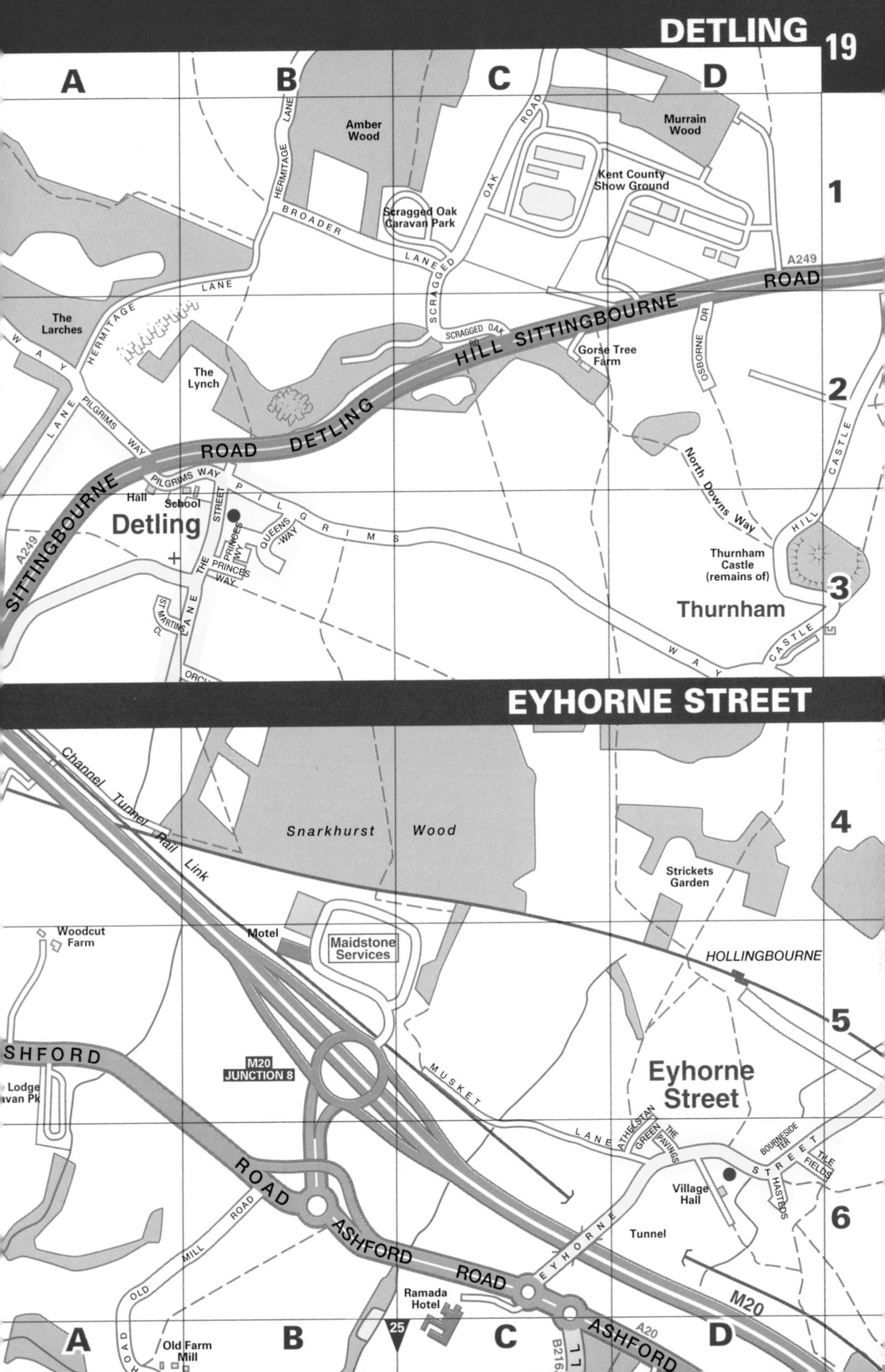

A   B   C   D

Amber Wood

Murrain Wood

Kent County Show Ground

OAK ROAD

BROADER LANE

HERMITAGE LANE

Scragged Oak Caravan Park

SCRAGGED LANE

1

LANE

A249

SITTINGBOURNE ROAD

HERMITAGE

The Larches

LANE

SCRAGGED OAK

HILL SITTINGBOURNE

Gorse Tree Farm

OSBORNE DR

2

The Lynch

DETLING

ROAD DETLING

WAY

PILGRIMS WAY

A249 SITTINGBOURNE

North Downs Way

CASTLE HILL

Hall School

PILGRIMS WAY

STREET

Detling

PILGRIMS WAY

QUEENS WAY

Thurnham Castle (remains of)

3

THE PRINCES WAY

LANE

ST MARTINS CL

Thurnham

WAY CASTLE

ORCH

Channel Tunnel Rail Link

Snarkhurst Wood

Strickets Garden

4

HOLLINGBOURNE

Woodcut Farm

Motel

Maidstone Services

5

SHFORD

Lodge van Pk

M20 JUNCTION 8

MUSKET

Eyhorne Street

LANE

ATHEASTAN GREEN THE PAVINGS

BOURNSIDE TER

STREET TILE FIELDS

ROAD

MILL ROAD

OLD ROAD

ASHFORD ROAD

EYHORNE ROAD

Village Hall

HASTEDS

STREET

6

Tunnel

Ramada Hotel

A20 ASHFORD

M20

A   B   C   D

ROAD

Old Farm Mill

25

B2163

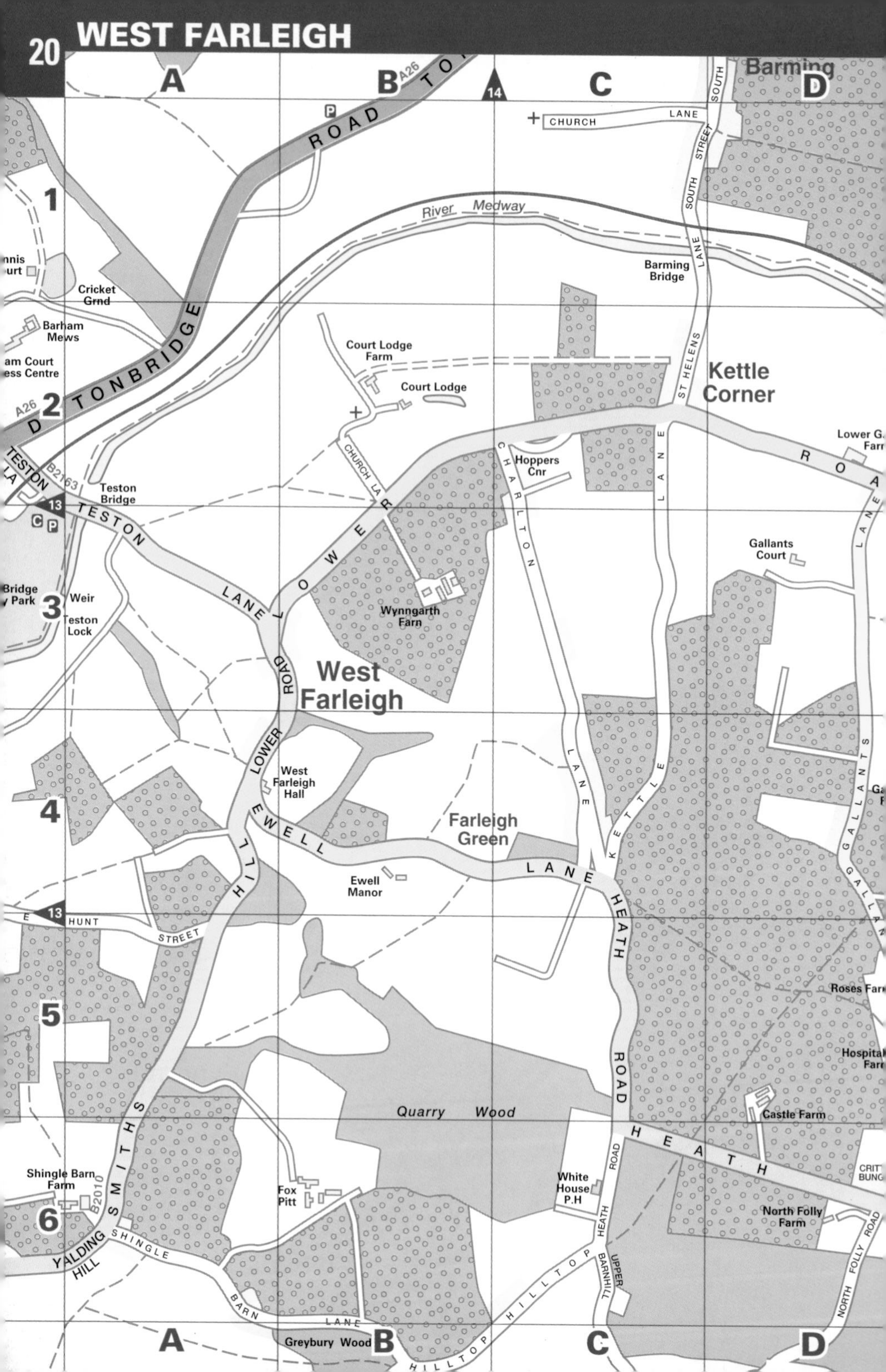

A B C D

Barming

1

River Medway

CHURCH LANE

SOUTH STREET

SOUTH LANE

Barming Bridge

Kettle Corner

Court Lodge Farm

Court Lodge

Hoppers Cnr

Lower G. Farr

Gallants Court

2

TONBRIDGE ROAD

A26

Tennis Court

Cricket Grnd

Barham Mews

am Court ess Centre

A26

TESTON LA

B2163

Teston Bridge

13

C P

TESTON

CHURCH LA

CHARLTON

ST HELENS LANE

LANE

ROA

3

Bridge y Park

Weir

Teston Lock

LANE

LOWER ROAD

Wynngarth Farn

West Farleigh

4

West Farleigh Hall

Farleigh Green

LANE

KETTLE

HEATH

GALLANTS

G.

Ga.

GALLAN

Ewell Manor

EWELL

HILH

13

HUNT STREET

LANE

ROAD

Roses Farm

Hospital Farm

5

SMITHS

Quarry Wood

Castle Farm

HEATH

CRIT BUNG

Shingle Barn Farm

B2010

Fox Pitt

White House P.H

North Folly Farm

6

YALDING HILL

SHINGLE

BARN

LANE

Greybury Wood

HILLTOP

HEATH ROAD

BARNHILL

UPPER

HILLTOP ROAD

NORTH FOLLY ROAD

A B C D

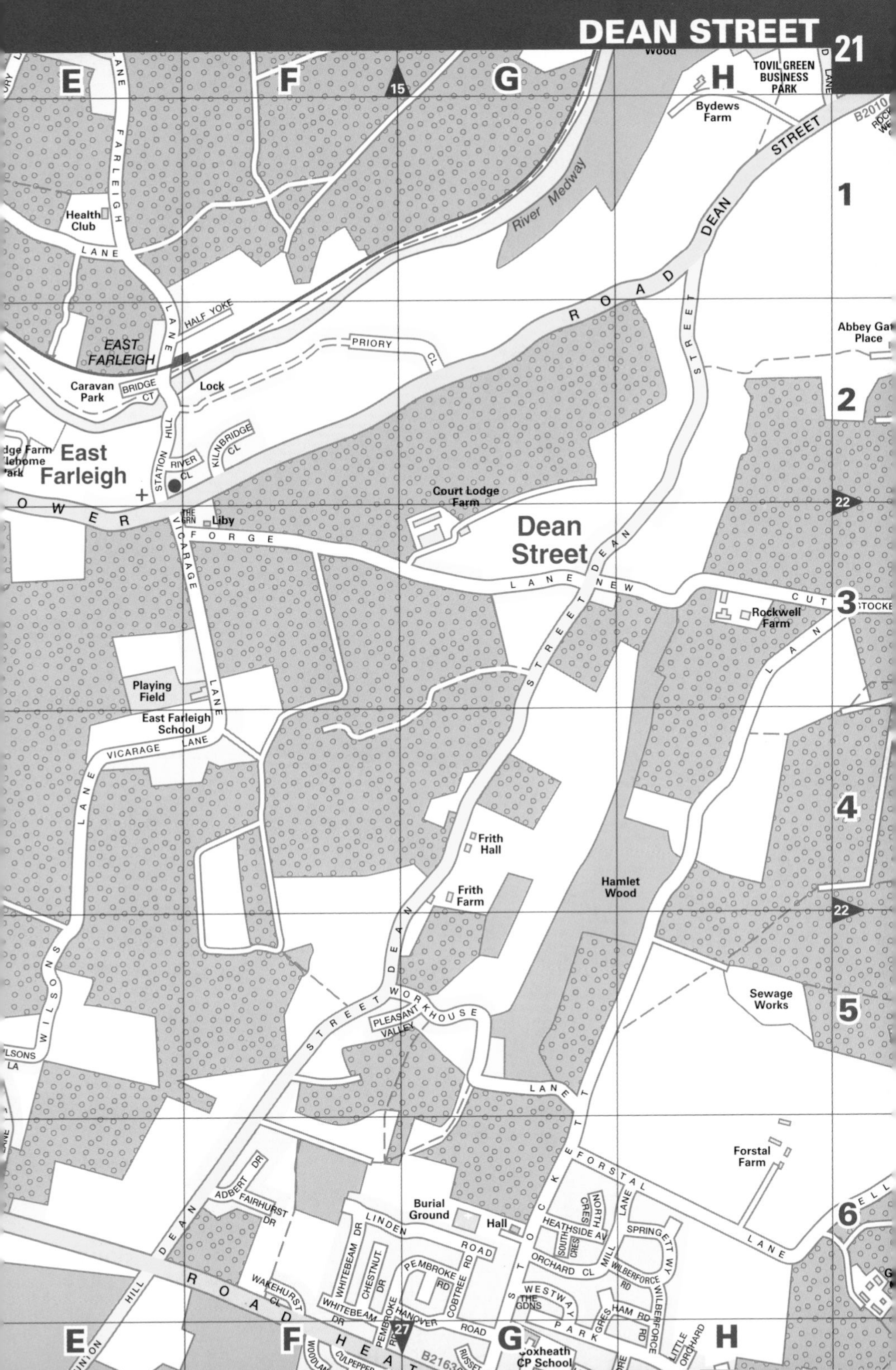

E F 15 G H 1

TOVIL GREEN
BUSINESS
PARK

Wood

Bydews
Farm

B2010

ROCH
WE

River Medway

ROAD

DEAN

STREET

Abbey Gate
Place

1

Health
Club

LANE

FARLEIGH LANE

HALF YOKE

EAST
FARLEIGH

PRIORY

CL

2

Caravan
Park

ge Farm
 lebome
ark

BRIDGE
CT

Lock

STATION HILL

RIVER CL

KILNBRIDGE CL

East
Farleigh

OWER

FORGE

VICARAGE

LANE

Liby

THE
RN

Court Lodge
Farm

Dean
Street

DEAN

NEW

CUT

STOCKE

22

Rockwell
Farm

3

STREET

LANE

LANE

N

Playing
Field

East Farleigh
School

VICARAGE LANE

4

Frith
Hall

Frith
Farm

Hamlet
Wood

22

WILSONS LA

DEAN

STREET

WORKHOUSE

PLEASANT
VALLEY

Sewage
Works

5

LANE

FORSTAL

Forstal
Farm

ELL

DEAN

ADBERT DR

FAIRHURST
DR

LINDEN

DR

WHITEBEAM DR

CHESTNUT DR

PEMBROKE
RD

Burial
Ground

Hall

ROAD

COITHE RD

HANOVER

ORCHARD CL

STOCKETT

HEATHSIDE AV

SOUTH
CRES

NORTH
CRES

MILL LANE

SPRINGETT WY

WILBERFORCE

WILBERFORCE RD

6

ROAD

HILL

WAKEHURST
CL

WHITEBEAM

PEMBROKE RD

CULPEPPER

WOODLAN

27

RUSSEL

WESTWAY

THE
GDNS

PARK

RD

GRES

HAM RD

LITTLE
ORCHARD

E F 27 G oxheath
CP School H

B2163

HEATH

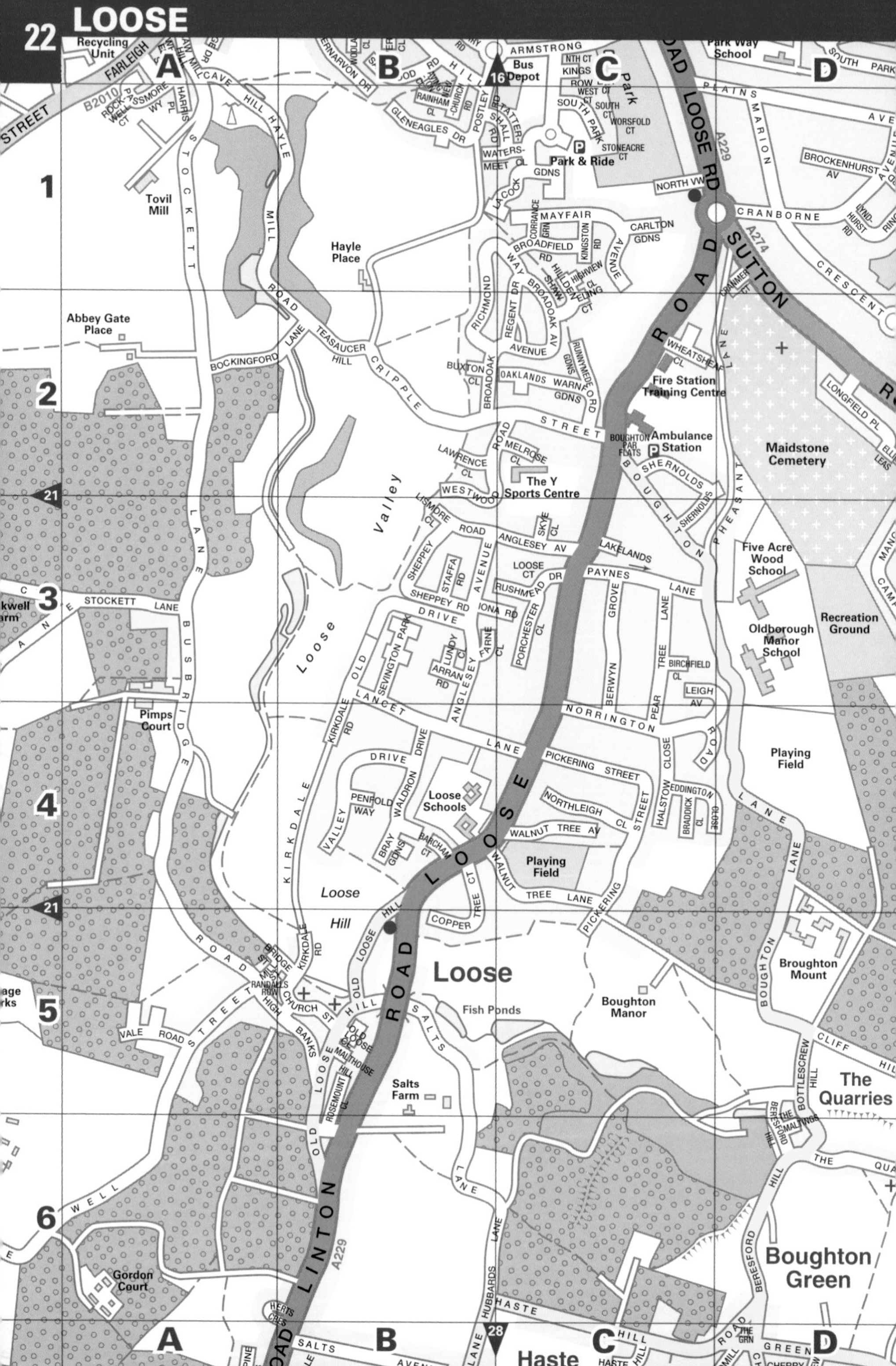
A
B
C
D
1
2
3
4
5
6
16
21
21
28
Recycling Unit
FARLEIGH
B2010
STREET
Tovil Mill
Bus Depot
ARMSTRONG
GLENEAGLES DR
RAINHAM CL
POSTLEY RD
Park & Ride
SOUTH PARK
WORSFOLD CT
STONEACRE CT
Park Way School
PLAINS
MARION
BROCKENHURST AV
NORTH VW
CRANBORNE
CRESCENT
SUTTON
A274
A229
LOOSE RD
MAYFAIR
CARLTON GDNS
BROADFIELD RD
KINGSTON RD
Hayle Place
HAYLE MILL ROAD
Abbey Gate Place
BOCKINGFORD LANE
TEASAUCER HILL
CRIPPLE STREET
RICHMOND WAY
REGENT DR
BROADOAK AV
BUXTON CL
OAKLANDS
RUNNYMEDE GDNS
WHEATSHEAF CL
Fire Station Training Centre
Ambulance Station
LONGFIELD PL
Maidstone Cemetery
STOCKETT LANE
LAWRENCE CL
MELROSE CL
The Y Sports Centre
WESTWOOD
Valley
LISMORE RD
ANGLESEY AV
LAKELANDS
SHERNOLDS
BOUGHTON
PHEASANT LANE
Five Acre Wood School
Recreation Ground
Oldborough Manor School
PAYNES LANE
LOOSE CT
RUSHMEAD DR
SHEPPEY RD
STAFFA RD
IONA RD
PORCHESTER CL
BERWYN GROVE
PEAR TREE LANE
BIRCHFIELD CL
LEIGH AV
Loose
SEVINGTON PARK
LUNDY CL
ARRAN RD
FARNE CL
LANCET LANE
KIRKDALE RD
NORRINGTON ROAD
BUSBRIDGE ROAD
Pimps Court
PICKERING STREET
Playing Field
Loose Schools
PENFOLD WAY
WALDRON DRIVE
VALLEY DRIVE
NORTHLEIGH CL
HALSTOW CLOSE
EDDINGTON CLOSE
BRADDICK CL
WALNUT TREE AV
BRAY GDNS
BARCHAM CT
Playing Field
WALNUT TREE LANE
COPPER TREE CT
Loose Hill
Loose
Fish Ponds
Boughton Manor
Broughton Mount
CHURCH ST
SALTS LANE
VALE ROAD
BANKS
MALTHOUSE HILL
ROSEMOUNT CL
Salts Farm
CLIFF HILL
BOTTLESCREW HILL
The Quarries
THE MALTINGS
BERESFORD HILL
WELL
Gordon Court
LINTON ROAD
HERTS CRES
HUBBARDS LANE
HASTE HILL
Boughton Green
Haste
SALTS AVENUE
GREEN
CHERRY

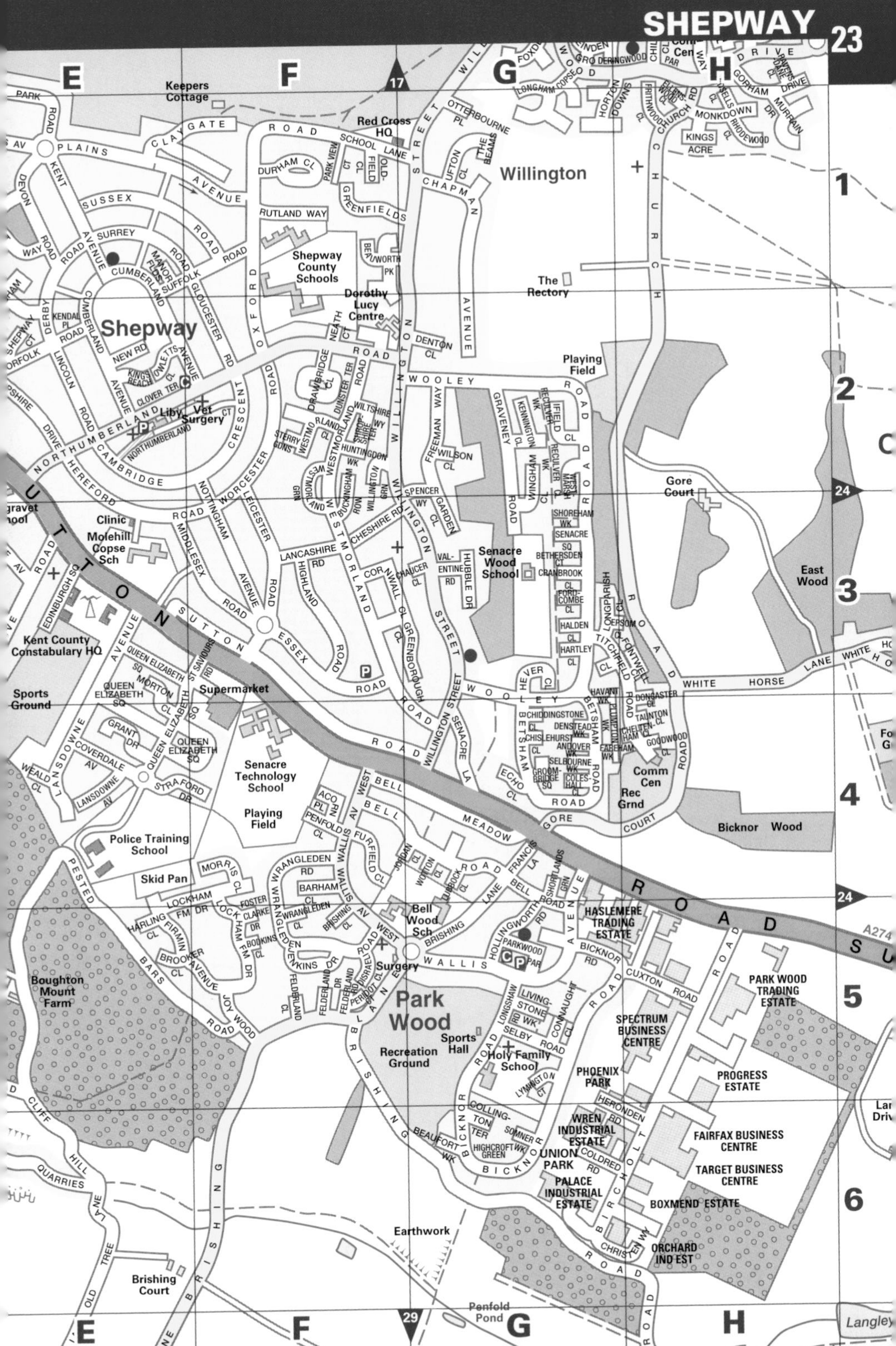
E
F
G
H
17
24
29
1
2
3
4
5
6
Keepers Cottage
Red Cross HQ
Willington
Shepway County Schools
Dorothy Lucy Centre
The Rectory
Playing Field
Shepway
Liby
Vet Surgery
Gore Court
East Wood
Clinic
Molehill Copse Sch
Senacre Wood School
Kent County Constabulary HQ
Sports Ground
Supermarket
Senacre Technology School
Playing Field
Comm Cen
Rec Grnd
Bicknor Wood
Police Training School
Skid Pan
Bell Wood Sch
Surgery
HASLEMERE TRADING ESTATE
PARK WOOD TRADING ESTATE
Boughton Mount Farm
Park Wood
Recreation Ground
Sports Hall
Holy Family School
SPECTRUM BUSINESS CENTRE
PHOENIX PARK
PROGRESS ESTATE
WREN INDUSTRIAL ESTATE
UNION PARK
FAIRFAX BUSINESS CENTRE
TARGET BUSINESS CENTRE
PALACE INDUSTRIAL ESTATE
BOXMEND ESTATE
ORCHARD IND EST
Earthwork
Brishing Court
Penfold Pond
Langley
SUTTON ROAD
WILLINGTON STREET
WOOLEY ROAD
CHURCH ROAD
WHITE HORSE LANE
PLAINS AVENUE
CLAYGATE ROAD
SCHOOL LANE
CHAPMAN AVENUE
OXFORD ROAD
NORTHUMBERLAND ROAD
CAMBRIDGE CRESCENT
WORCESTER ROAD
WESTMORLAND ROAD
ESSEX ROAD
GREENBOROUGH CL
SENACRE LA
BETSHAM ROAD
GORE COURT ROAD
BELL ROAD
MEADOW
BICKNOR ROAD
CUXTON ROAD
BIRCHOLT ROAD
BRISHING LANE
BRISHING ROAD
BARS
JOY WOOD
WRANGLEDEN RD
WALLIS AV
DEEP CLIFF

A
B
C
D
1
2
3
4
5
6
18
23
23
30
Caring
Caring Farm
Fulling Mill Farm
Little Caring Farm
CARING ROAD
CARING LANE
Green Hill
GREEN HILL
OTHAM STREET
Village Green
Spout Farm
Merriams Farm
STONEACRE LANE
Hall
Stoneacre N.T.
Stoneacre Farm
Otham
FORGE LANE
BACK STREET
East Wood
OTHAM
HOLLY FARM ROAD
Holly Farm
SIMMONDS LA
WHITE HORSE LA
HONEY LANE
White Horse P.H.
Football Ground
Belts Wood
Cricket Ground
AVERY LANE
NEW ROAD
Otham Hole
Wood
Rumwood Court
A274
SUTTON ROAD
Nursery
Pleydells Farm
Langley
Hall
Butlers Farm
Rec Grnd
Surgery
HORSESHOES LANE
Langley Corner Farm
The Horseshoes P.H.
Langley Park Driving Range
Langley Park Farm
HEATH ROAD
TURGIS CL
PORTERS WK
LACEY CL
GULLANDS
COPPERFIE
DR
SKINNERS WAY
DICKENS CLOSE
FORSTERS
SHEPHERDS WAY
ORCHARD CL
Sunrise Pre Prep Sch
St Marys
Green Lane Farm
GREEN LANE
LEEDS ROAD
B2163
ULCOMBE
Langley Loch
Weir

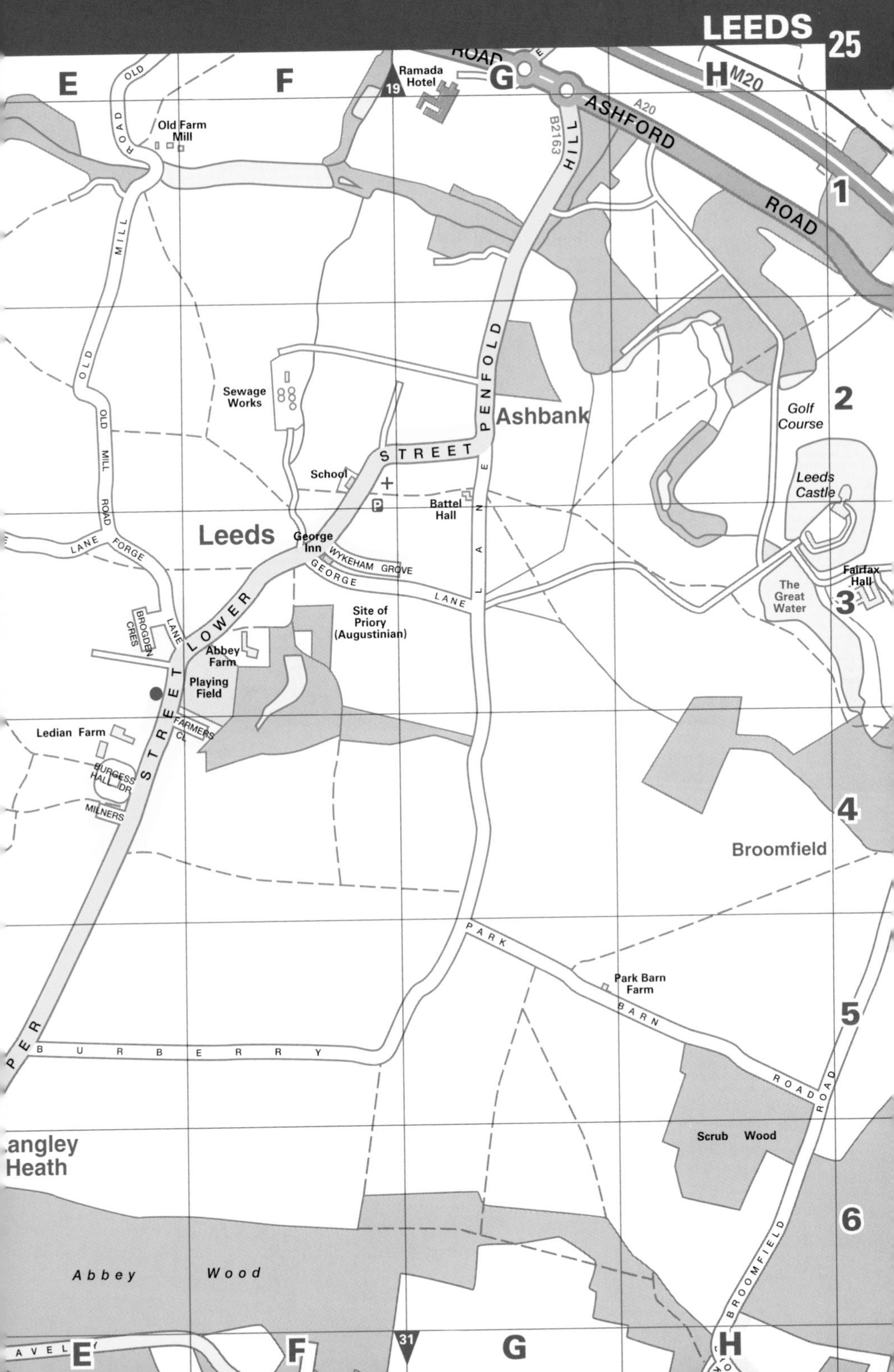
E
F
G
H
Ramada Hotel
19
M20
A20
ASHFORD ROAD
ROAD
B2163
HILL
OLD ROAD
Old Farm Mill
OLD MILL
1
Sewage Works
PENFOLD
Ashbank
2
Golf Course
STREET
School
Leeds Castle
Battel Hall
LANE
Leeds
George Inn
WYKEHAM GROVE
GEORGE LANE
FORGE LANE
OLD MILL ROAD
Fairfax Hall
The Great Water
3
Site of Priory (Augustinian)
BROGDEN CRES
LANE
LOWER
Abbey Farm
Playing Field
STREET
Ledian Farm
FARMERS CL
BURGESS HALL DR
MILNERS
4
Broomfield
PARK
Park Barn Farm
BARN
5
UPPER
BURBERRY
ROAD
ROAD
Scrub Wood
Langley Heath
6
BROOMFIELD
Abbey Wood
E
F
31
G
H

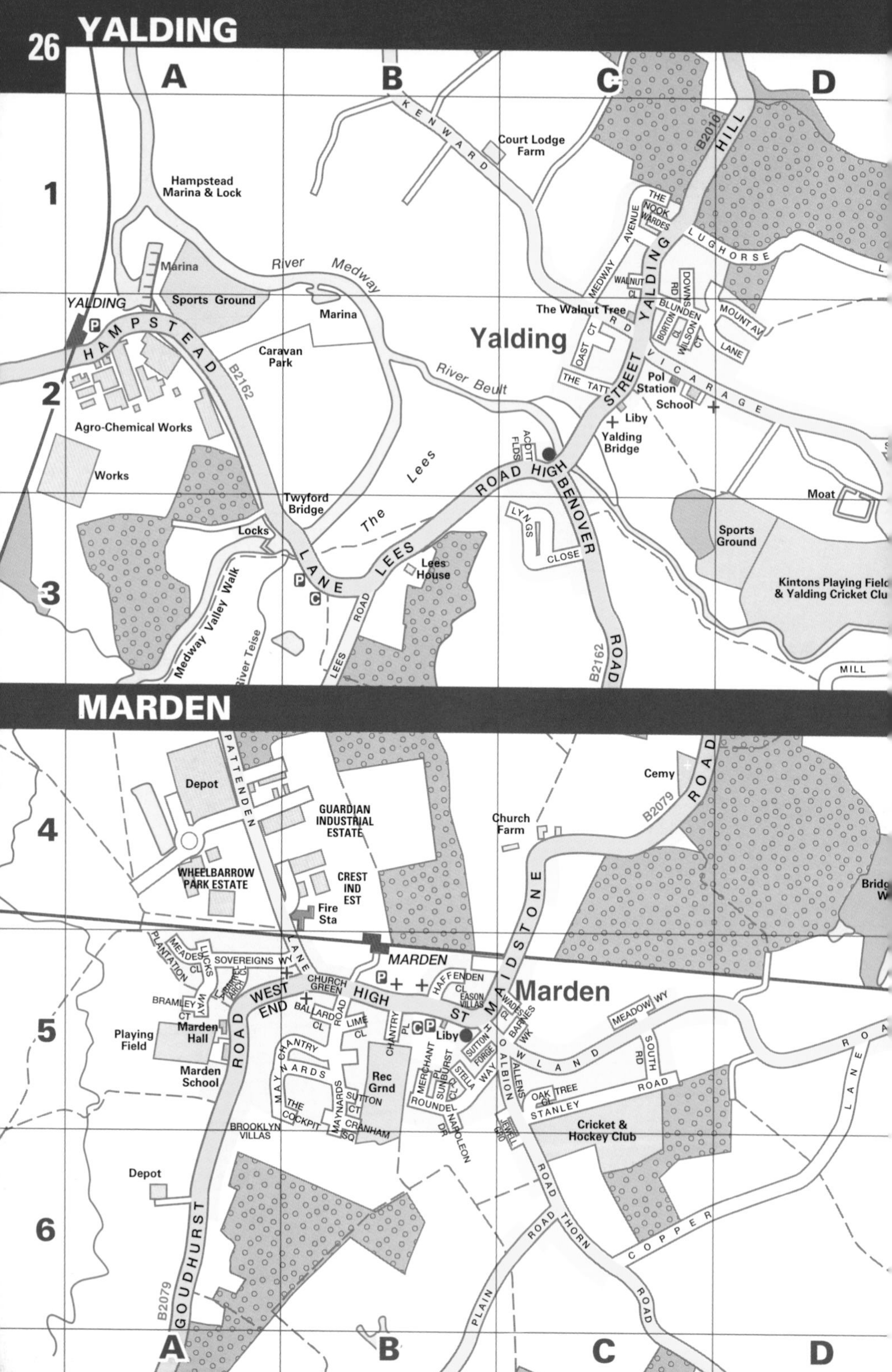

YALDING

A   B   C   D

1

Hampstead Marina & Lock

Court Lodge Farm

KENWARD

B2010 HILL

Hampstead Marina & Lock

THE NOOK
WARDES

MEDWAY AVENUE

LUGHORSE

Marina

River Medway

YALDING

HAMPSTEAD

Sports Ground

Marina

Caravan Park

B2162

The Walnut Tree

WALNUT

YALDING STREET

OAST CT RD

BLUNDEN

BORTON

WILSON

DOWNSWOOD

RD

MOUNT AV

LANE

Yalding

2

Agro-Chemical Works

River Beult

THE TATT

Pol Station

VICARAGE

Liby

School

Works

Twyford Bridge

The Lees

Locks

LANE

LEES ROAD

ROAD HIGH

BENOVER

Yalding Bridge

LYNGS

CLOSE

Moat

Sports Ground

3

Medway Valley Walk

River Teise

LEES LANE

LEES ROAD

P C

Lees House

B2162 ROAD

Kintons Playing Field & Yalding Cricket Clu

MILL

MARDEN

4

PATTENDEN

Depot

GUARDIAN INDUSTRIAL ESTATE

Cemy

Church Farm

B2079 ROAD

WHEELBARROW PARK ESTATE

CREST IND EST

Fire Sta

Bridg W

5

MEADES

LOCKS

CL

WAY

SOVEREIGNS WY

LANE

CHURCH GREEN

MARDEN

HIGH ST

HAFFENDEN

EASON VILLAS

Marden

MAIDSTONE

MEADOW WY

BRAMLEY CT

WEST END ROAD

BALLARDS CL

LIME CL

P

Liby

CHANTRY PL

C P

SUTTON

FORGE

STELLA

ALLENS WAY

WADES

BARNES

WK

SOUTH RD

ROA

Playing Field

Marden Hall

Marden School

MAYNARDS

THE COCKPIT

CHANTRY

MERCHANT

SUNBURST

ROUNDEL

NAPOLEON

OAK TREE

STANLEY

ROAD

Rec Grnd

SUTTON CT

CRANHAM SQ

BROOKLYN VILLAS

Cricket & Hockey Club

LANE

6

Depot

GOUDHURST ROAD

B2079

PLAIN ROAD

ROAD THORN

COPPER ROAD

ROAD

A   B   C   D

A **B** **C** **D**

1

2

3 into

4

5

6

UPPER HUNTON HILL ROAD

HEATH ROAD

AMSBURY

Earthworks

Amsbury Wood

Reason Hill

Amsbury Farm

Old Savage

WOODLANDS

WAKEHAM CL

WHITEBEAM DR

WHITE...

PEMBRE... DR

CHESS... RD

DOVER

COBTREE RD

ROAD

B2163

HUNTINGTON RD

CLINTON RD

CULPEPPER

RD

HUNTINGTON CL

BURSTON RD

PIPPIN

CL

CAPELL

ROAD

WAVERLEY RD

CRISPIN CT

DANE CT

THE BEACONS

RUSSET CT

MAF...

ELMFIELD CT

P

Coxheath Centre

Amb H.Q.

Orchard Medical Centre

WESTWAY

THE ...

PARK

Coxheath CP School

Physiotherapy Centre

Liby

Day Centre

LINTON

GORE

BRAM... BRAM...

LIBERS RD

GEORGIAN...

ADAM PL

GRESHAM RD

WILBERFORCE

...FORCE RD

LITTLE ORCHARD

THE VALLEY

ASPIAN

WAY

DRIVE

B2163

ROAD

H

Coxheath

Clock House Farm

WESTERHILL ROAD

WESTERHILL ROAD

Westerhill Farm

BARNES

LACEYS

LANE

VANITY LANE

VANITY LANE

28

WHEELERS

CORNWALLIS AV

28

STREET

WALL

ED

Martins Farm House

Burford Farm

BONFLOWER LANE

Wares Farm

River Farm

Ware Farm

LANE

REDWALL

River Beult

Landing Strip

A **B** **C** **D**

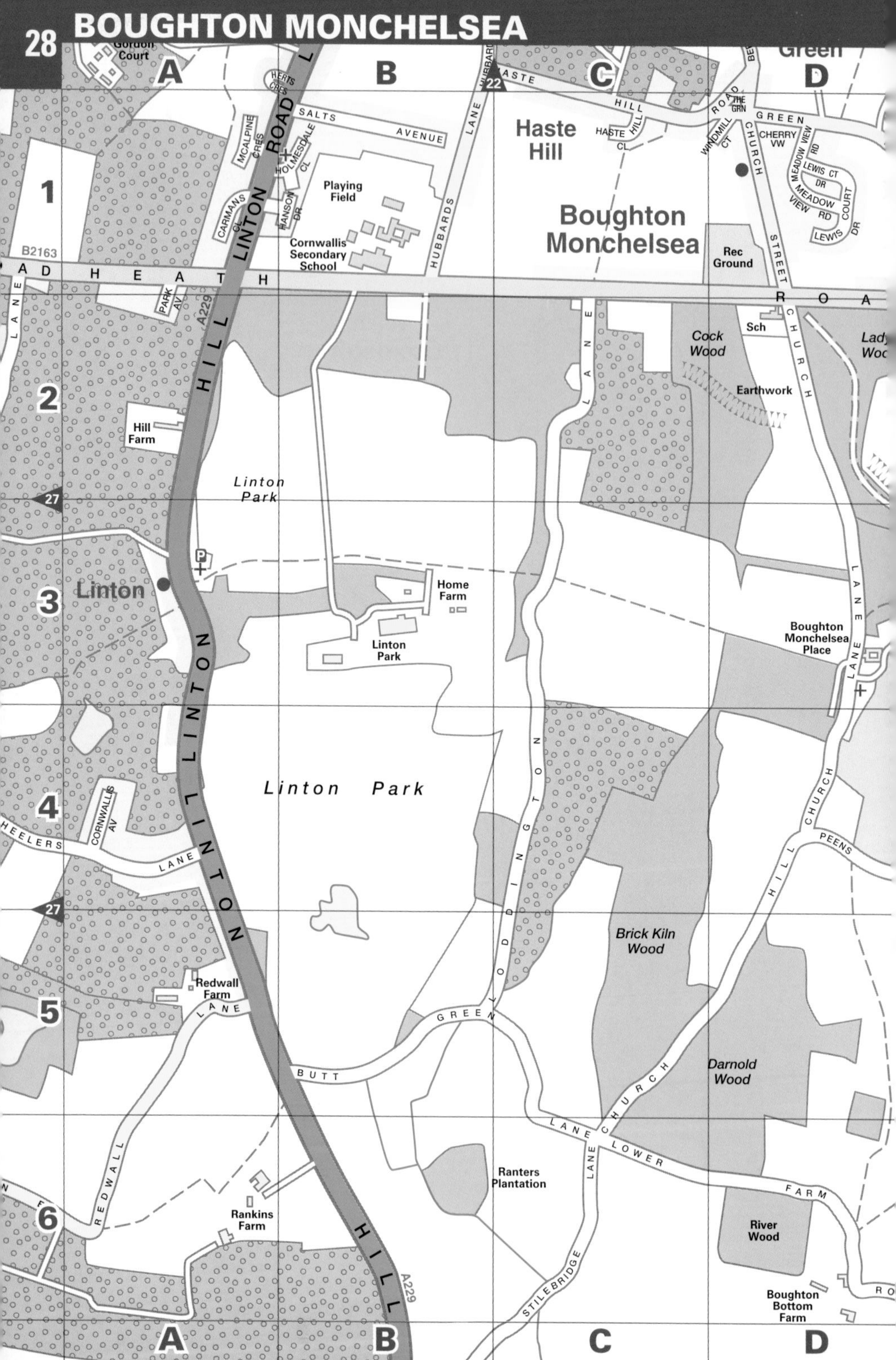

Green

Gordon Court

A **B** **C** **D**

Haste Hill

HILL

Haste Hill CL

Boughton Monchelsea

SALTS

AVENUE

Playing Field

Cornwallis Secondary School

HUBBARDS

B2163

A D H E A T H

HILL ROAD

LINTON ROAD

MCALPINE CRES

HOLMESDALE CL

CARMANS

PARK AV

A229

HERTS CRES

THE GRN

CHURCH STREET

GREEN

CHERRY VW

MEADOW VIEW DR

LEWIS CT DR

MEADOW VIEW RD

COURT DR

LEWIS

Rec Ground

R O A

Cock Wood

Sch

Earthwork

Lady Wood

Hill Farm

2

1

Linton Park

27

3 Linton

Home Farm

Linton Park

Boughton Monchelsea Place

LINTON LANE

HEELERS

CORNWALLIS AV

4

Linton Park

CHURCH HILL

PEENS

27

5

Redwall Farm

LANE

Brick Kiln Wood

GREEN

LODDINGTON

CHURCH LANE

Darnold Wood

BUTT

Ranters Plantation

CHURCH LOWER

FARM

River Wood

REDWALL

Rankins Farm

HILL A229

STILEBRIDGE LANE

Boughton Bottom Farm

6

A **B** **C** **D**

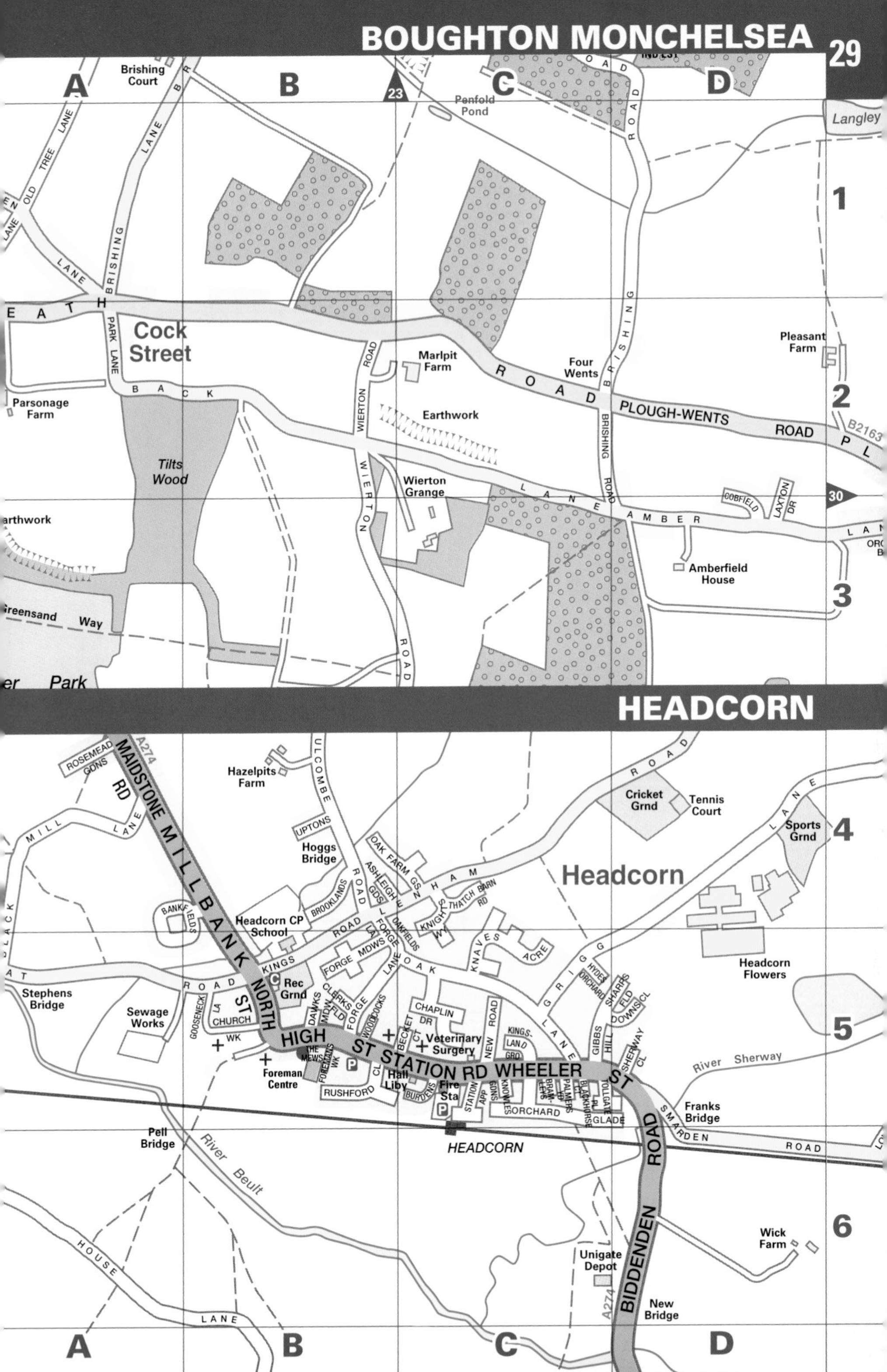

A   **B**   **C**   **D**

Brishing Court

Langley

Penfold Pond

Cock Street

Marlpit Farm

Four Wents

Pleasant Farm

PLOUGH-WENTS ROAD

B2163

Parsonage Farm

Earthwork

Wierton Grange

earthwork

Tilts Wood

GOBFIELD

LAXTON DR

Amberfield House

Greensand Way

Park

1

2

3

30

HEADCORN

ROSEMEAD GDNS

MAIDSTONE RD

A274

MILLBANK NORTH ST

Hazelpits Farm

ULCOMBE

Cricket Grnd

Tennis Court

Sports Grnd

Headcorn

MILL LANE

UPTONS

Hoggs Bridge

OAK FARM CL

ASHLEIGH

BANKFIELDS

Headcorn CP School

KINGS

Rec Grnd

Stephens Bridge

Sewage Works

GOOSENECK ROAD

CHURCH

WK

HIGH ST

STATION RD WHEELER ST

Veterinary Surgery

CHAPLIN DR

KINGS LAND GRO

Headcorn Flowers

River Sherway

Foreman Centre

THE MEWS

RUSHFORD

Fire Sta

HEADCORN

ORCHARD

Franks Bridge

SMARDEN ROAD

Pell Bridge

River Beult

BIDDENDEN ROAD

A274

Unigate Depot

New Bridge

Wick Farm

HOUSE LANE

4

5

6

A   **B**   **C**   **D**

Langley Loch   Weir

A   B   24   C   D

1

Rectory Farm

Five Wents   The Plough P.H   LEEDS

Pleasant Farm   Fir Tree Farm   COLLINGWOOD INDUSTRIAL ESTATE

2   ROAD   B2163   PLOUGH - WENTS   MAIDSTONE

CHART SUTTON BUSINESS ESTATE

LESTED LANE

AMBER WY   Chart Corner   WARMLAKE INDUSTRIAL ESTATE   STREET

29   LAXTON DR   ORCHARD BANK   LANE   WARMLAKE   NORTON ROAD   ROAD   CHARTWAY

3   Chart Sutton   MARSHAM CRES   Rec Grnd   Warmlake   Sutton Valence Nursing & Care Centre

MERCER WY   HILL   CHURCH ROAD   Sports Ground

4   CHART   Haven Farm   Rec Ground

CHURCH RD   Court Farm   Sports Ground

Sch   CHURCH RD   Greensand   Way   School   SOUTHWAYS   Sutton Valence School   NORTH STREET

SCHOOL LANE   HIGH STREET   Lby   BROAD   RECTOR

5   Park House Farm   ROAD   LOWER RD   THE PLATT   HEADCORN RD

Rectory Farm   SOUTH BANK   Surg

Coombe Farm   CAPTAINS PL

6   Pond   FORSHAM   LANE   THE HARBOUR   SOUTH   HEADCORN RD   A274

A   B   C   D

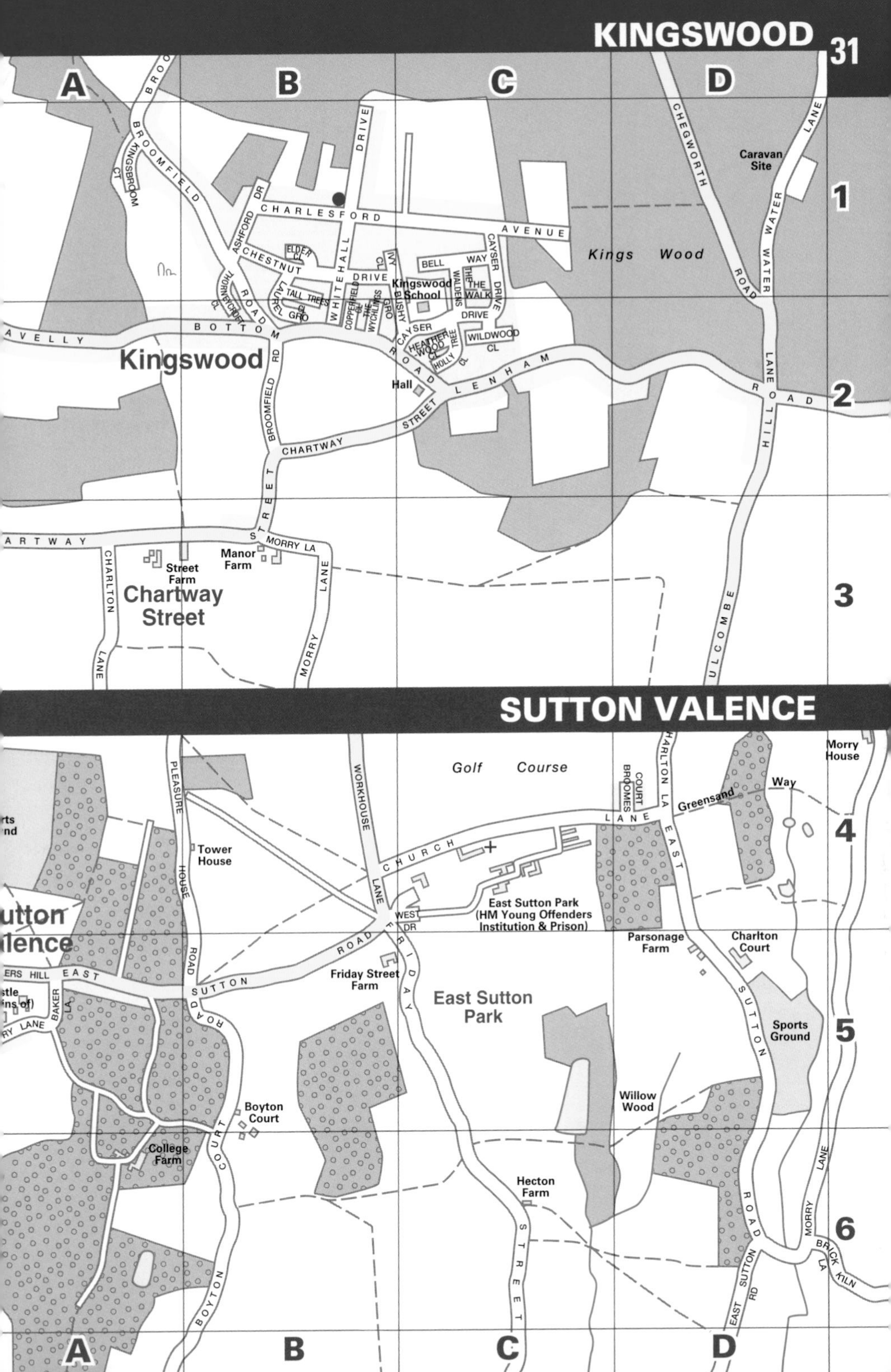

KINGSWOOD

A · B · C · D

1 · 2 · 3

Caravan Site

BROOMFIELD

KINGSBROOM CT

BROOMFIELD DRIVE

ASHFORD DR

CHARLESFORD

DRIVE

CHESTNUT

ELDER CL

TALL TREES

THE GRO

WHITEHALL

COPPERFIELD DRIVE

IVY BUSH DR

THE WICHES

THE WALDENS

BELL

WAY

CAYSER DRIVE

AVENUE

Kings Wood

CHEGWORTH

WATER LANE

WATER LANE

HILL ROAD

Kingswood

BOTTOM

AVELLY

Kingswood School

HEATHER WOOD CL

HOLLY CL

WILDWOOD CL

THE WALK

CAYSER ROAD

Hall

LENHAM STREET

BROOMFIELD RD

CHARTWAY

STREET

ULCOMBE

ARTWAY

CHARLTON LANE

Street Farm

Manor Farm

MORRY LA

MORRY LANE

Chartway Street

SUTTON VALENCE

Golf Course

Morry House

PLEASURE

WORKHOUSE LANE

CHURCH LANE

CHARLTON LA

COURT BROOMES

EAST

Greensand

Way

Tower House

+

East Sutton Park
(HM Young Offenders
Institution & Prison)

utton
alence

HOUSE ROAD

SUTTON

WEST DR

FRIDAY

ROAD

Parsonage Farm

Charlton Court

ERS HILL

stle ns of)

RY LANE

BAKER LA

EAST

Friday Street Farm

East Sutton Park

SUTTON ROAD

Sports Ground

COURT

Boyton Court

Willow Wood

College Farm

Hecton Farm

EAST SUTTON RD

MORRY LANE

BRICK KILN

BOYTON

STREET

4 · 5 · 6

A · B · C · D

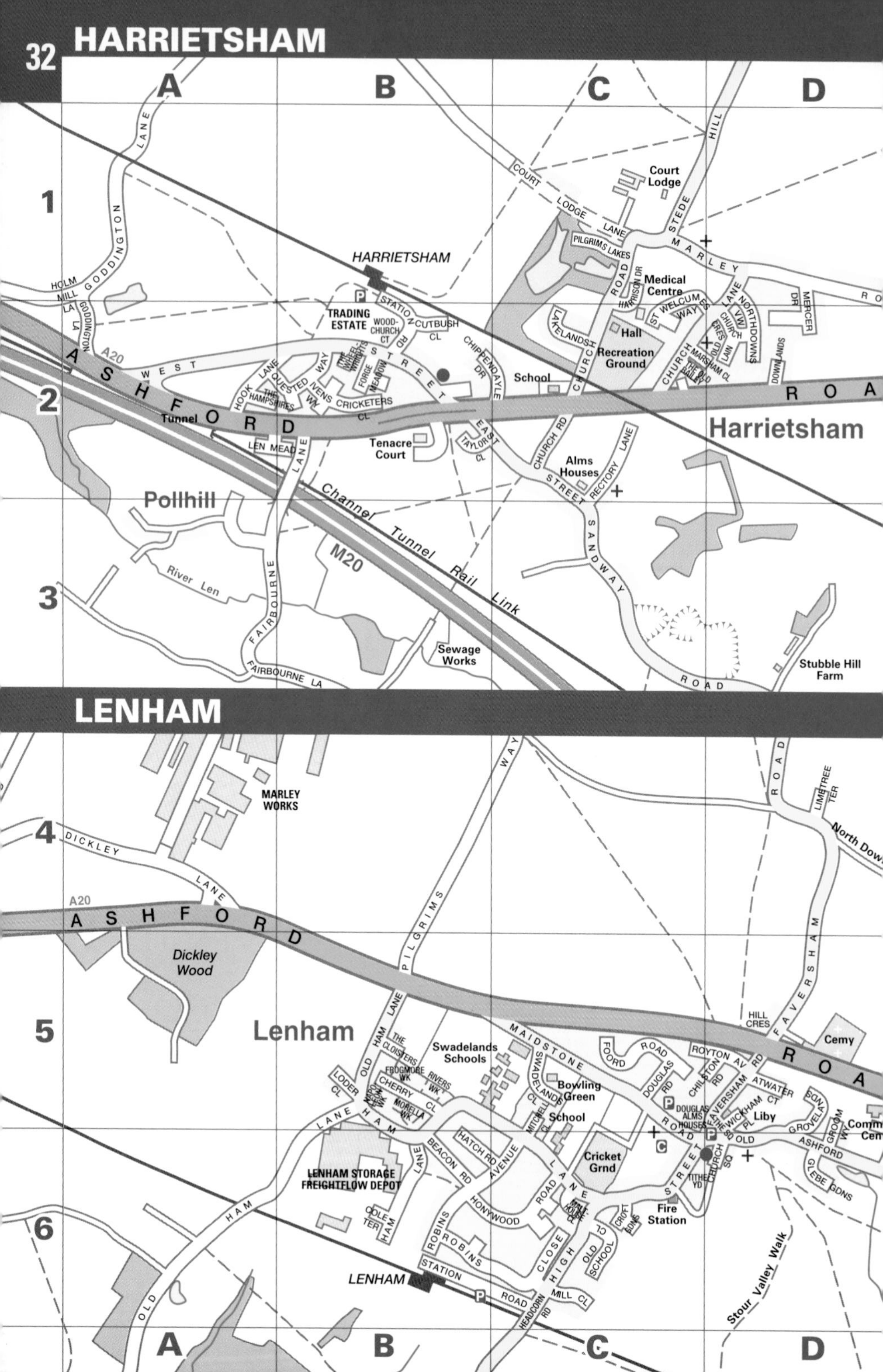

LENHAM

A   **B**   **C**   **D**

1

2

3

4

5

6

Court Lodge

PILGRIMS LAKES

Medical Centre

HARRIETSHAM

TRADING ESTATE

WOOD-CHURCH CT

CUTBUSH CL

Hall

Recreation Ground

School

Harrietsham

Tunnel

THE HAMPSHIRES

CRICKETERS CL

LEN MEAD

Tenacre Court

Alms Houses

Pollhill

Channel Tunnel Rail Link

M20

River Len

FAIRBOURNE LA

Sewage Works

Stubble Hill Farm

MARLEY WORKS

DICKLEY LANE

A20

ASHFORD

Dickley Wood

Lenham

Swadelands Schools

Bowling Green

School

Cricket Grnd

LENHAM STORAGE FREIGHTFLOW DEPOT

Fire Station

DOUGLAS ALMS HOUSES

Liby

Cemy

Comm Cen

Stour Valley Walk

LENHAM

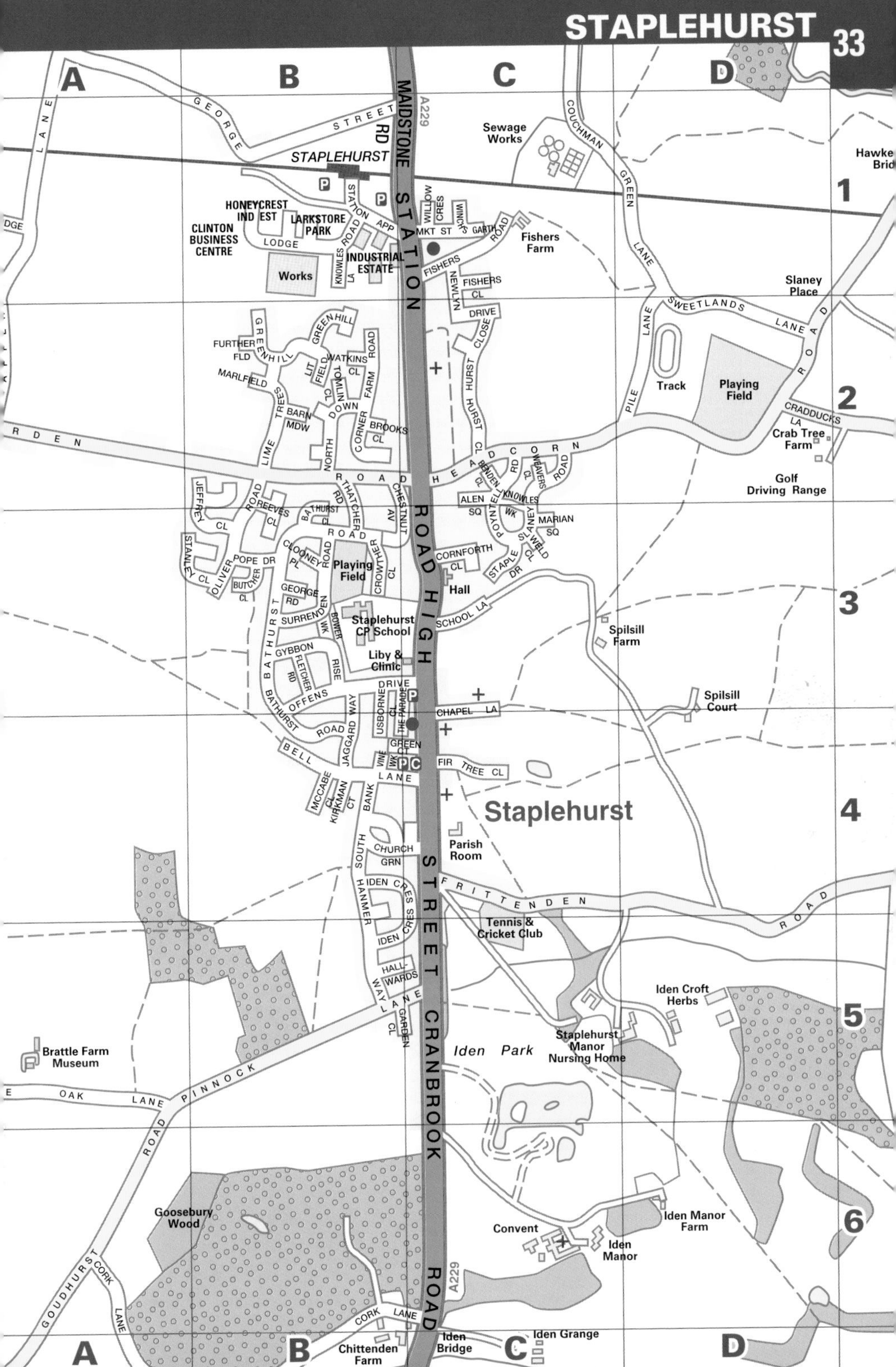

Grid references: A B C D across the top and bottom; 1 2 3 4 5 6 down the right side.

STAPLEHURST
MAIDSTONE RD
A229
GEORGE STREET
Sewage Works
COUCHMAN GREEN
Hawke Bridge
HONEYCREST IND EST
LARKSTORE PARK
CLINTON BUSINESS CENTRE
LODGE
Works
INDUSTRIAL ESTATE
STATION APP
WILLOW CRES
MKT ST
NEWS
GARTH ROAD
WINGS
Fishers Farm
Slaney Place
STATION ROAD
KNOWLES LA
FISHERS
FISHERS DRIVE
CLOSE
HURST RD
SWEETLANDS LANE
PILE LANE
Track
Playing Field
CRADDUCKS LA
Crab Tree Farm
GREEN HILL
GREENHILL
FURTHER FLD
MARLFIELD
WATKINS CL
DOWNTON
LITT FIELD
FARM ROAD
BARN MDW
CORNER FARM
NORTH
BROOKS CL
LIME TREES
HEAD CORN ROAD
WEAVERS RD
Golf Driving Range
JEFFREY CL
REEVES CL
THATCHERS CL
BA'HURST
CHESTNUT AV
CROWTHER RD
ALEN SQ
POYNTON
KNOWLES WK
MARIAN SQ
STANLEY CL
OLIVER CL
POPE DR
BUTCHER
CLOONEY PL
GEORGE RD
SURRENDEN
Playing Field
CORNFORTH CL
STAPLE SLANEY DR
S WELD
MARIAN SQ
Hall
Staplehurst CP School
Liby & Clinic
GYBBON RD
FLETCHER RD
OFFENS
BATHURST ROAD
USBORNE CL
DRIVE
THE PARK
GREEN
CHAPEL LA
Spilsill Farm
Spilsill Court
BELL
JAGGARD WAY
VINE
SPC
FIR TREE CL
MCCABE CT
KIRKMAN CT
BANK
LANE
Staplehurst
SOUTH
CHURCH GRN
Parish Room
HANMER
IDEN CRES
Tennis & Cricket Club
HALL WARDS
WAY LANE
IDEN CL
GARDEN CL
FRITTENDEN ROAD
Iden Croft Herbs
Brattle Farm Museum
Iden Park
Staplehurst Manor Nursing Home
Iden Manor Farm
OAK LANE
PINNOCK
GOUDHURST
CORK LANE
Goosebury Wood
Convent
Iden Manor
CRANBROOK STREET ROAD
A229
CORK LANE
Chittenden Farm
Iden Bridge
Iden Grange

The Index includes some names for which there is insufficient space on the maps. These names are indicated by an * and are followed by the nearest adjoining thoroughfare.

Cheriton Way ME16   9 G6
Cherry Cl ME17   32 B5
Cherry Orch ME20   8 A5
Cherry Orch Way ME16   15 F5
Cherry Vw ME17   28 D1
Chervilles ME16   15 E6
Cheshire Rd ME15   23 F3
Chesterton Rd ME20   7 G1
Chestnut Av TN12   33 B2
Chestnut Cl ME19   12 D3
Chestnut Dr, Coxheath ME17   21 F6
Chestnut Dr, Kingswood ME17   31 B1
Chestnut Walk ME20   7 H3
Cheviot Gdns ME15   17 H6
Chiddingstone Cl ME15   23 G4
Chilham Rd ME16   9 G6
Chillington St ME14   16 B1
Chilston Rd ME17   32 C5
Chiltern Cl ME15   17 H6
Chippendayle Dr ME17   32 B2
Chipstead ME16   15 G2
Chislehurst Cl ME15   23 G4
Christen Way ME15   23 G6
Christie Dr ME20   7 F1
Church Cres ME17   32 D2
Church Fld ME6   4 D2
Church Flds ME19   6 C5
Church Grn, Marden TN12   26 B5
Church Grn, Staplehurst TN12   33 B4
Church Hill ME17   28 C6
Church La, Barming ME16   20 C1
Church La, Bearsted ME14   18 B4
Church La, Boughton Monchelsea ME17   28 D2
Church La, East Sutton ME17   31 B4
Church La, Harrietsham ME17   32 C2
Church La, West Farleigh ME15   20 B2
Church Rd, Chart Sutton ME17   30 B4
Church Rd, Harrietsham ME17   32 C2
Church Rd, Maidstone ME15   16 A6
Church Rd, Offham ME19   5 C5
Church Rd, Otham ME15   23 H1
Church Rd, Ryarsh ME19   6 A2
Church Sq ME17   32 D6
Church St, Boughton Monchelsea ME17   28 D1
Church St, Loose ME15   22 B5
Church St, Maidstone ME14   3 D2
Church St, Teston ME18   13 F1
Church St, Tovil ME15   16 A6
Church St West ME18   13 E2
Church Walk, Ashford TN27   29 F5
Church Walk, Aylesford ME20   9 E3
Church Walk, West Malling ME19   7 G6
Churchfield ME19   5 B2
Churchill Ho ME16   15 F6
Churchill Sq ME19   12 D3
Clapper La TN12   33 A2
Clare La ME19   7 E5
Clare Wood Dr ME19   7 F5
Claremont Rd ME14   3 F1
Clarence Ct ME14   17 F3
Clarendon Cl ME14   17 H4
Clarendon Pl ME14   3 E3
Clark Mws ME20   8 D5
Claygate ME15   23 E1
Cleeve Ct ME19   12 E3
Clemens Pl ME19   12 E4
Clement Ct ME16   15 H2
Clerks Fld TN27   29 F5
Cleveland Ho ME16   15 F6
Clewson Rise ME14   10 D6
Cliff Hill ME17   23 E5
Cliff Hill Rd ME17   22 D5
Clifton Cl ME14   16 D2
Clinton Cl ME17   27 B1

Cliveden Cl ME16   9 H6
Clock Tower Mws ME6   4 C1
Clooney Pl TN12   33 B3
Cloudberry Cl ME16   15 H2
Clover Ter ME15   23 E2
Coach Yd ME16   15 F5
Cobbett Cl ME19   7 F4
Cobbs Cl ME18   13 C2
Cobdown Cl ME20   8 A3
Cobfield ME17   29 H2
Cobham Cl ME16   16 A3
Cobham Dr ME19   12 F3
Cobtree Rd ME17   21 G6
Coldharbour La ME20   9 E5
Coldred Rd ME15   23 G6
Cole Ter ME17   32 B6
Colegate Dr ME14   18 B3
Coleridge Cl ME20   7 G1
Coleshall Cl ME15   23 G4
Coll Cotts ME15   16 B5
College Av ME15   16 B5
College Rd, Aylesford ME20   8 A2
College Rd, Maidstone ME15   16 B5
College Walk ME15   16 B5
Collinge Cl ME19   7 G4
Collington Ter ME15   23 G6
Collingwood Ind Est ME17   30 D2
Colman Par ME14   3 D3
Coltsfoot Dr ME14   17 G3
Columbine Cl ME19   7 G4
Columbine Rd ME19   7 G4
Command Rd ME14   10 B5
Commodore Rd ME14   16 D2
Comp La ME19   5 A6
Connaught Cl ME15   23 G5
Consort Cl ME14   16 D3
Constitution Hill ME6   4 B2
Conway Rd ME16   15 F1
Coombe Cl ME14   17 E1
Coombe Rd ME15   16 B6
Cooper Rd ME6   4 B5
Copper La TN12   26 C6
Copper Tree Ct ME15   22 B5
Copperfield Cl ME17   31 B2
Copperfield Dr ME17   24 D6
Coppice Vw ME14   17 F2
Copsehill ME19   7 F3
Copsewood Way ME15   17 H5
Corben Cl ME15   15 E2
Coriander Dr ME16   15 E4
Cork La TN12   33 A6
Corner Farm Rd TN12   33 B2
Cornflower Cl ME14   17 F4
Cornforth Cl TN12   33 C3
Cornwall Cl ME15   23 F3
Cornwall Av ME17   28 A4
Cornwallis Rd ME16   15 H4
Corona Ter ME6   4 B5
Corrall Ct ME14   3 F2
Corrance Grn ME15   22 C1
Cotswold Gdns ME15   17 H6
Cottenham Cl ME19   7 G6
Couchman Green La TN12   33 C1
Coulters Cl ME14   17 F3
County Gro ME19   6 C5
County Rd ME14   3 C1
Court Broomes ME17   31 D4
Court Dr ME16   15 H3
Court Lodge ME18   13 F2
Court Lodge La ME17   32 C1
Courtenay Rd ME15   16 A6
Courtlands ME18   13 E1
Courtlands Cl ME18   13 F1
Coverdale Av ME15   23 E4
Covey Hall Rd ME6   4 C2
Cowden Rd ME14   17 E2
Cowdrey Cl ME16   15 F6
Cox Ct ME19   12 E3
Coxs Cl ME6   4 B2
Crabtree Cl ME14   12 C4
Cradducks La TN12   33 D2
Cranborne Av ME15   22 D1
Cranbrook Cl ME15   23 G3
Cranbrook Rd TN12   33 C5
Cranham Sq TN12   26 B5
Cranleigh Gdns ME16   9 G6
Cranmer Ct ME15   22 D2
Crayford Cl ME14   16 D2
Crest Ind Est TN12   26 B4

Creve Coeur Cl ME14   17 H2
Cricketers Cl ME17   32 B2
Cripple St ME15   22 B2
Crismill La ME14   18 D5
Crispin Cl ME17   27 C1
Crispin Way ME18   12 D3
Crittenden Bglws ME15   20 D6
Croft Gdns ME17   32 C6
Crompton Gdns ME15   3 E4
Cromwell Rd ME14   3 E2
Cronin Cl ME20   7 G1
Cross Keys ME14   18 B4
Cross St ME14   16 B1
Crownfields ME14   17 G3
Crowther Cl TN12   33 B3
Crundale ME14   3 E2
Cuckoowood Av ME14   10 B5
Cudham Cl ME14   17 E2
Culpepper Rd ME17   27 B1
Cumberland Av ME15   23 E1
Curzon Rd ME14   16 C1
Cut Bush Cl ME17   32 B2
Cutbush Ct ME14   3 F2
Cuxton Rd ME15   23 H5
Cygnet Cl ME20   7 H3

Dane Cl ME17   27 C1
Danefield Ct ME14   18 B4
Danns La ME19   12 D4
Dargate Cl ME16   9 G6
Dawks Mdw TN27   29 F5
Dawn La ME19   12 F3
Deacon Trading Est ME20   9 E3
Dean St ME15   21 E6
Deerhurst Gdns ME16   15 H4
Delamere Gdns ME6   4 C2
Delamere Rd ME6   4 C2
Denning Cl ME16   15 F3
Dennis Cadman Ho ME20   8 D5
Denstead Walk ME15   23 G4
Denton Cl ME15   23 G2
Derby Rd ME15   23 E2
Deringwood Dr ME15   17 G6
Deringwood Par ME15   17 G6
Detling Hill ME14   19 B2
Devon Rd ME15   23 E1
Dhekelia Cl ME16   10 B6
Dickens Cl ME17   24 D6
Dickens Dr ME19   7 F4
Dickens Rd ME14   10 A6
Dickley La ME17   32 A4
Discovery Dr ME19   12 D3
Discovery Rd ME15   18 A5
Disraeli Cl ME15   23 F5
Ditton Court Cl ME20   8 A5
Ditton Pl ME20   8 A4
Dixon Cl ME15   16 B5
Doddington Cl ME16   16 A3
Doncaster Cl ME15   23 H4
Dorset Way ME15   23 E1
Douglas Alms Houses ME17   32 C5
Douglas Rd, Lenham ME17   32 C5
Douglas Rd, Maidstone ME16   16 A5
Dover St ME16   15 G5
Dowling Cl ME6   4 A3
Downderry Way ME20   7 H3
Downlands ME17   32 D2
Downs Cl, Ashford TN27   29 H5
Downs Cl, Maidstone ME14   10 C5
Downs Rd, Penenden Heath ME14   10 C6
Downs Rd, Yalding ME18   26 C1
Downs Vw ME19   6 C5
Downs Vw Rd ME14   10 C6
Drawbridge Cl ME15   23 F2
Dryland Rd ME6   4 B3
Duchess of Kent Ct ME20   8 D5
Dukes Walk ME15   3 D4
Dunera Cl ME15   16 B5
Dunster Ter ME15   23 F2
Durham Cl ME15   23 F1

Eagle Cl ME20   7 G2
Earl St ME14   3 B3
Eason Villas TN12   26 B5
East Ct ME15   16 C6

East Park Rd ME20   9 E5
East St, Maidstone ME17   32 B2
East St, Snodland ME6   4 D3
East St, West Malling ME19   5 C2
East St North ME19   5 C1
East Sutton Rd ME17   31 A5
Easterfields ME19   14 A3
Eastfield Ho ME16   15 F6
Eastry Cl ME16   9 G6
Eastwell Cl ME14   16 D2
Ebony Walk ME15   15 F4
Eccleston Rd ME15   16 A5
Echo Cl ME15   23 G4
Eddington Cl ME15   22 C4
Eden Farm Rd ME19   6 D5
Edgar Pl ME15   3 D3
Edgeler Ct ME16   4 B4
Edinburgh Sq ME15   23 E3
Edmund Cl ME16   15 E4
Edna Rd ME14   10 A6
Edward Walk ME19   7 G5
Egerton Rd ME15   10 A6
Egremont Rd ME15   17 G5
Elder Cl ME17   31 B1
Eling Ct ME15   22 C2
Elizabeth Smith Ct ME19   7 F6
Ellenswood Cl ME15   17 H6
Ellingham Leas ME15   22 D2
Elm Cres ME17   7 G5
Elm Gro ME15   16 C5
Elm Walk ME20   8 C4
Elmfield Ct ME17   27 C1
Elmstone Cl ME16   15 F5
Elmstone La ME16   15 E5
Elstar Pl ME19   12 D3
Elvington Cl ME15   15 H3
Emsworth Gro ME14   17 E1
Enterprise Rd ME15   22 C1
Epsom Cl, Maidstone ME15   23 G3
Epsom Cl, West Malling ME19   6 B4
Erith Cl ME14   10 C6
Ernest Dr ME16   15 F2
Essex Rd ME15   23 F3
Euroway ME20   8 C6
Evelyn Rd ME16   15 H4
Evergreen Cl ME19   7 E3
Eversley Cl ME15   15 G1
Ewell Av ME19   6 B5
Ewell La ME15   20 A4
Exton Gdns ME14   17 G2
Eyhorne St ME17   19 C6
Eylesden Ct ME14   18 B4
Eynsford Rd ME16   9 H6

Fairbourne La ME17   32 A3
Fairfax Bsns Centre ME15   23 H6
Fairhurst Dr ME15   21 F6
Fairlawn Cl ME14   13 E1
Fairmeadow ME14   3 B1
Falcon Grn ME20   7 F3
Fallowfield Cl ME14   17 G4
Fant La ME16   15 F5
Faraday Rd ME14   10 D6
Fareham Walk ME15   23 G4
Faringdon Cl ME15   15 F4
Farleigh Cl ME15   15 E6
Farleigh Hill ME16   16 A6
Farleigh La ME16   15 E6
Farmer Cl ME17   25 E4
Farnborough Cl ME16   15 G6
Farne Cl ME15   22 B3
Farningham Cl ME14   17 E1
Farrier Cl ME14   17 F3
Fartherwell Av ME19   6 B4
Fartherwell Rd ME19   6 A6
Farthings Cotts ME14   10 B4
Fauchons Cl ME14   17 G4
Fauchons La ME14   17 H4
Faversham Rd ME17   32 D5
Fawley Cl ME15   16 A1
Felderland Cl ME15   23 F5
Felderland Dr ME15   23 F5
Felderland Rd ME15   23 F5
Fennel Cl ME16   15 F4
Fernhill Rd ME16   15 E6
Fernleigh Rise ME20   7 H3
Ffinch Cl ME20   8 B6
Fielding Dr ME20   7 G1
Fields La ME18   13 C2
Fiji Ter ME14   10 C6

Finch Ct ME14   10 A6
Finglesham Ct ME15   23 E2
Fintonagh Dr ME14   16 C1
Firmin Av ME15   23 E5
Firs Cl ME20   8 C4
Firs La ME17   18 D6
Firtree Cl TN12   33 C4
Fisher St ME14   16 B2
Fishers Cl TN12   33 C1
Fishers Rd TN12   33 C1
Fitzwilliam Rd ME14   17 G3
Five Oak La TN12   33 A5
Flaxman Dr ME15   15 G1
Fletcher Rd TN12   33 B3
Flood Hatch ME15   15 H6
Florence Rd ME16   16 A5
Flower Rise ME14   16 B1
Flume End ME16   15 H6
Foley St ME14   3 E1
Fontwell Cl ME15   23 H3
Foord Rd ME17   32 C5
Fordcombe Cl ME15   23 H3
Fordingbridge Cl ME16   15 F2
Fordwich Cl ME16   9 H6
Foremans Barn Rd ME15   27 A1
Foremans Walk TN27   29 B5
Forest Hill ME15   16 B6
Forest Way ME19   12 C3
Forge La, Ashford TN27   29 F5
Forge La, Boxley ME14   11 E3
Forge La, East Farleigh ME15   21 F3
Forge La, Leeds ME17   24 D2
Forge Mdw ME17   32 B2
Forge Mdws TN27   29 F5
Forsham La ME17   30 C6
Forstal Cotts ME20   9 F3
Forstal La ME17   21 G6
Forstal Rd ME20   9 E3
Forsters ME17   24 C6
Forsyth Cl ME17   7 G4
Fortune Way ME19   12 E3
Foster Clark Est ME16   16 D5
Foster Clarke Dr ME15   23 F5
Foster St ME15   16 B4
Fountain La ME16   15 E5
Four Acres ME19   14 A2
Foxden Dr ME15   17 G6
Foxglove Rise ME14   16 A1
Francis La ME15   23 G4
Franklin Dr ME14   17 F4
Freelands Rd ME16   4 A3
Freeman Way ME15   23 G2
Fremlin Walk Shopping Centre ME15   3 C2
Fremlins Rd ME14   18 B3
Freshland Rd ME16   15 F3
Friars Ct ME14   3 E3
Friars Vw ME20   8 C3
Friday St ME17   31 B5
Frinstead Walk ME16   15 F1
Frithwood Cl ME15   17 H6
Frittenden Rd TN12   33 C4
Frog La ME19   6 D5
Frogmore Walk ME17   32 B5
Froyle Cl ME16   15 G1
Fulbert Dr ME14   17 H2
Fullers Cl ME14   17 H3
Furfield Cl ME15   23 F4
Further Fld TN12   33 B2

Gabriels Hill ME15   3 D3
Gagetown Ter ME14   16 B1
Gainsborough Dr ME16   15 F3
Gallants La ME15   20 D4
Gandys La ME17   29 E1
Garden Cl, Maidstone ME15   23 G3
Garden Cl, Tonbridge TN12   33 B5
Garden Way ME19   12 C4
Garner Dr ME19   7 H4
Garrington Cl ME14   17 E1
Gascoyne Ct ME15   18 A6
Gassons Rd ME6   4 A3
Gatcombe Cl ME16   15 F3
Gatland La ME16   15 E6
Gault Cl ME15   17 H6
Gentian Cl ME14   17 F3
George La ME17   25 F3
George St, Hunton ME15   27 A5
George St, Maidstone ME15   16 C5

ieorge St, Tonbridge TN12 33 B1
ieorgian Dr ME17 27 D1
iibbs Hill, Ashford TN27 29 G5
iibbs Hill, Maidstone ME18 13 A3
iibraltar La ME14 10 A5
iibson Dr ME19 12 C2
iiddy Horn La ME16 15 G3
iighill Rd ME20 7 G1
iilbert Ter ME14 16 B1
iladstone Rd ME14 16 B1
ileaners Dr ME14 17 F4
ilebe Gdns ME17 32 D6
ilebe La ME16 14 D6
ilebe Mdw ME18 13 C2
ileneagles Dr ME15 22 B1
ilenleigh Rd ME18 13 B3
ilenwood Cl ME16 15 G3
iloucester Rd ME15 23 F1
iodden Rd ME6 4 B3
ioddington La ME17 32 A1
ioldfinch Cl ME20 7 G2
iolding Cl ME20 8 B4
ioldings Cl ME19 12 D4
ioldthorne Cl ME14 16 D3
iooch Cl ME16 9 H6
ioodmans Mews ME18 13 C2
ioodwin Dr ME14 10 D6
ioodwood Cl ME15 23 H4
iooseneck La TN27 29 F5
iore Court Rd ME15 23 G4
iorham Cl ME6 4 B3
iorham Dr ME15 17 H6
iorse Cres ME20 8 B6
ioudhurst Cl ME16 16 A3
ioudhurst Rd, Marden TN12 26 A6
ioudhurst Rd, Staplehurst TN12 33 A6
irace Av ME16 15 G2
irampian Way ME15 17 H6
iranada St ME15 3 D4
iranary Cl ME14 17 F2
irange Cl ME19 6 C3
irange La ME14 10 B4
irant Dr ME15 23 E4
iranville Rd ME14 16 B1
irapple Rd ME14 10 B6
irasslands ME17 24 D6
irassmere ME19 7 F3
iravelly Bottom Rd ME17 31 A2
iraveney Rd ME15 23 G2
irebe Ct ME20 7 F3
irecian St ME14 16 C2
ireen Ct TN12 33 B4
ireen Hill ME15 24 A1
ireen La, Boughton Monchelsea ME17 28 D1
ireen La, Langley ME17 24 D6
ireen Way ME16 15 F4
ireenborough Cl ME15 23 G3
ireenfields ME15 23 F1
ireenhill TN12 33 B2
ireenhithe ME15 16 B5
ireensands Rd ME15 17 H6
ireenside ME15 3 F4
ireensleeves Way ME19 12 F3
ireenways ME14 17 G2
ireenwich Cl ME16 15 H3
irenadier Cl ME15 17 G6
iresham Rd ME17 27 C1
irey Wethers ME14 10 A2
ireyfriars Cl ME16 15 H3
ireystones Rd ME15 17 H5
irigg La TN27 29 G5
iroom Way ME17 32 D5
iroombridge Sq ME15 23 G4
irosvener Ct ME16 15 G5
irove Green La ME14 17 G3
irove Green Rd ME14 17 G3
irove Rd ME15 23 E3
irovelands ME17 32 D5
irovewood Ct ME14 17 F4
irovewood Dr North ME14 17 F2
irovewood Dr South ME14 17 F4
iuardian Ind Est TN12 26 B4
iullands ME17 24 D5
iuston Rd ME14 16 D2
Guys Ct ME19 12 C3
Gybbon Rise TN12 33 B3

Hackney Rd ME16 15 G6
Hadlow Rd ME14 16 D2
Haffenden Cl TN12 26 B5
Halden Cl ME15 23 G3
Half Yoke ME16 21 F2
Halfpenny Cl ME16 15 E5
Hall Rd ME20 8 D5
Hallwards TN12 33 B5
Halstead Walk ME16 9 G6
Halstow Cl ME15 22 C4
Ham La ME17 32 B5
Hambledon Ct ME16 15 F5
Hammonds Sq ME6 4 C3
Hampden Way ME19 12 B3
Hampshire Dr ME15 22 D2
Hampson Way ME14 17 H3
Hampstead La ME18 26 A2
Hampton Rd ME14 16 D1
Hanbury Cl ME18 13 C2
Hanmer Way TN12 33 B4
Hanover Grn ME20 7 F1
Hanover Rd ME17 21 F6
Hanson Dr ME15 28 B1
Harbourland Cl ME14 10 D5
Hardie Cl ME19 7 F4
Hardy St ME14 16 B2
Harebell Cl ME14 17 F3
Harling Cl ME15 23 E5
Harp Farm Rd ME14 11 E1
Harple La ME14 11 G5
Harris Pl ME15 22 A1
Harrison Dr ME17 32 C2
Harrow Way ME14 17 G2
Harrower Dr ME15 16 D5
Hart St ME16 3 B4
Hart St Commercial Centre ME16 16 A5
Hartley Cl ME15 23 G3
Hartnup St ME16 15 G5
Harvest Ridge ME19 7 E3
Harvesters Way ME14 17 F3
Haslemere Trading Est ME15 23 G5
Haste Hill Cl ME17 28 C1
Haste Hill Rd ME17 22 C6
Hasteds ME17 19 D6
Hastings Rd ME15 3 E4
Hatch Rd ME17 32 B6
Hatherall Rd ME14 16 C2
Havant Walk ME15 23 G3
Hawkridge Gro ME19 12 D3
Hawkwood ME16 15 F3
Hawthornden Cl ME19 12 F3
Haydon Cl ME16 15 F4
Hayes Walk ME19 12 D4
Hayfield ME19 7 E3
Hayle Mill Rd ME15 22 A1
Hayle Rd ME15 16 B5
Hayrick Cl ME14 17 G2
Hays Rd ME6 4 A4
Haywain Cl ME14 17 G3
Hazel Av ME16 15 G2
Hazelwood Dr ME16 15 F3
Hazen Rd ME19 12 E3
Hazlitt Dr ME16 15 H2
Headcorn Rd, Lenham ME17 32 C6
Headcorn Rd, Sutton Valence ME17 30 D6
Headcorn Rd, Tonbridge TN12 33 C2
Headingley Rd ME16 15 F1
Heaf Gdns ME20 8 D5
Heath Gro ME16 15 E5
Heath Rd, Boughton Monchelsea ME17 28 A1
Heath Rd, Coxheath ME17 27 B1
Heath Rd, Langley ME17 24 D6
Heath Rd, Maidstone ME16 14 D5
Heath Rd, West Farleigh ME15 20 C4
Heathcote Cl ME20 8 D3
Heather Dr ME15 16 C6
Heatherwood Cl ME17 31 C2
Heathfield ME17 24 D6
Heathfield Av ME14 11 E6
Heathfield Cl ME14 16 D1
Heathfield Rd ME14 16 D1
Heathorn St ME14 3 E1
Heathside Av ME17 21 G6
Hedley St ME14 3 E1
Henbane Cl ME14 17 F2
Hendy Rd ME6 4 D2
Hengist Ct ME14 3 E3
Henley Flds ME14 17 F2
Henrys Cl ME18 13 B3
Hereford Rd ME15 23 E2
Hermitage Ct ME16 14 D3
Hermitage La, Aylesford ME20 8 D6
Hermitage La, Detling ME14 19 B1
Hermitage La, Maidstone ME16 15 E2
Heron Rd ME20 7 F3
Heronden Rd ME15 23 G5
Herts Cres ME15 22 A6
Hever Cl ME15 23 G3
Hever Gdns ME16 16 A5
Hewitt Cl ME16 9 H6
Hextable Cl ME16 9 G6
High Banks ME15 22 A5
High St, Ashford TN27 29 F5
High St, Aylesford ME20 8 D3
High St, East Malling ME19 7 G6
High St, Lenham ME17 32 C6
High St, Maidstone ME14 3 B4
High St, Marden TN12 26 B5
High St, Snodland ME6 4 C2
High St, Staplehurst TN12 33 C3
High St, Sutton Valence ME17 30 D5
High St, West Malling ME19 6 C5
High St, Yalding ME18 26 C2
Higham Cl ME15 15 H6
Higham Vw ME14 10 A2
Highberry ME19 7 F3
Highcroft Grn ME15 23 G6
Highland Rd ME15 23 F3
Highridge Cl ME14 17 G3
Highview Cl ME15 22 C1
Hildenborough Cres ME16 9 F6
Hill Brow ME14 17 H3
Hill Cres ME17 32 D5
Hillary Rd ME14 10 C6
Hillden Shaw ME15 22 C1
Hillside Ct ME18 13 C2
Hockers Cl ME14 11 H5
Hockers La ME14 11 H6
Hodgson Cres ME6 4 C2
Hog Hill ME14 18 A3
Holborough Rd ME6 4 C2
Holland Rd ME14 3 E1
Hollingworth Rd ME15 23 G5
Hollondbury Pk ME19 12 F4
Hollow La ME6 4 A4
Holly Farm Rd ME15 24 C4
Holly Gdns ME14 16 D1
Holly Tree Cl ME17 31 C2
Holmesdale Cl ME15 28 B1
Holmoaks ME14 17 E3
Holt Wood Av ME20 8 C5
Holtye Cres ME15 16 C6
Honduras Ter ME14 16 C1
Honey La ME15 24 A3
Honeycrest Ind Est TN12 33 B1
Honywood Rd ME17 32 B6
Hook La ME17 32 A2
Hook Rd ME6 4 B2
Hope St ME14 16 B2
Hornbeam Cl ME20 7 H3
Horseshoe Cl ME14 17 G2
Horseshoes La ME17 24 C6
Horton Downs ME15 23 G1
Howard Dr ME16 15 F2
Howard Rd ME19 7 F4
Howick Cl ME20 8 D5
Howland Rd TN12 26 B5
Hubbards La ME17 22 B6
Hubble Dr ME15 23 G3
Hunt St ME15 13 C4
Huntingdon Walk ME15 23 F2
Huntington Rd ME17 27 B1
Hunton Hll ME15 27 A2
Huntsman La ME14 16 D3
Hurricane Rd ME19 12 B3
Hurst Cl TN12 33 C2
Hurst Way ME16 14 D6
Huxley Cl ME20 7 G2
Hyde Rd ME16 15 H1
Hydes Orch TN27 29 G5

Iden Cres TN12 33 B4
Ifield Cl ME15 23 G2
Imperial Cl ME19 12 D3
Industrial Distribution Centre ME6 4 B4
Ingle Pl ME19 12 D4
Iona Rd ME15 22 B3
Ivens Way ME17 32 B2
Ivy Cl ME17 31 B1

Jaggard Way TN12 33 B4
Jamaica Ter ME14 16 B1
James St ME14 3 D1
James Whatman Way ME14 3 B1
Jasmine Cl ME19 7 G4
Jasmine Rd ME19 7 G4
Javelin Rd ME19 12 B3
Jeffrey Cl TN12 33 B2
Jeffrey St ME14 3 D2
Jenkins Dr ME15 23 F5
Jerome Rd ME20 7 F1
Jewell Gro TN12 26 C5
John St ME14 16 B1
Jordan Cl ME15 23 F4
Joy Wood ME15 23 F5
Juniper Cl ME16 15 F1

Keats Rd ME20 7 G2
Kendal Pl ME15 23 E2
Kendall Av ME19 12 E3
Kenilworth Ho ME16 15 F6
Kennington Cl ME15 23 G2
Kent Av ME15 23 E1
Kent Rd ME6 4 C4
Kent St ME18 12 A4
Kentish Ct ME16 3 A3
Kenward Rd, Maidstone ME16 15 G3
Kenward Rd, Yalding ME18 26 B1
Kenya Ter ME14 16 B1
Kerry Hill Way ME14 16 A1
Keswick Dr ME16 15 F3
Kettle La ME15 20 C4
Kewlands ME14 17 E2
Kiln Barn Rd ME20 8 A5
Kilnbridge Cl ME15 21 F2
Kilndown Cl ME16 9 G6
King Edward Rd ME15 16 B6
King Hill ME19 12 D1
King St, Maidstone ME15 3 D3
King St, West Malling ME19 6 C5
Kingfisher Mdw ME16 16 B5
Kingfisher Rd ME20 7 F3
Kings Acre ME15 23 H1
Kings Hill Av ME19 12 C2
Kings Rd TN27 29 F5
Kings Reach ME15 23 E2
Kings Row ME15 16 C6
Kings Walk ME14 3 F2
Kingsbroom Ct ME17 31 A1
Kingsdown Cl ME16 16 A3
Kingsgate Cl ME16 15 G3
Kingsland Gro TN27 29 G5
Kingsley Rd ME15 3 E4
Kingston Rd ME15 22 C1
Kipling Dr ME20 7 F1
Kirkdale ME15 22 B4
Kirkdale Rd ME15 22 B5
Kirkman Ct TN12 33 B4
Knaves Acre TN27 29 G5
Knightrider Ct ME15 3 D4
Knightrider St ME15 3 D4
Knights Way TN27 29 G4
Knott Ct ME14 16 B1
Knowle Rd ME14 16 C1
Knowles Gdns TN27 29 G5
Knowles La TN12 33 B1
Knowles Walk TN12 33 C2
Knowlton Gdns ME16 15 F5

Laburnum Dr ME20 7 H3
Lacey Cl ME17 24 D6
Laceys La ME17 27 C4
Lacock Gdns ME15 22 B1
Lacy Cl ME16 9 H6
Ladds La ME6 4 C1
Lake Rd ME20 8 C6
Lake Walk ME20 4 C6
Lakelands, Harrietsham ME17 32 C2
Lakelands, Maidstone ME15 22 C3
Lakeside ME6 4 B5
Lakeview Cl ME6 4 C5
Lamberhurst Rd ME16 9 F6
Lambert Mws ME6 4 C2
Lambourne Dr ME19 12 C4
Lambourne Rd ME15 17 G5
Lancashire Rd ME15 23 F3
Lancaster Way ME19 12 C3
Lancet La ME15 22 B3
Langdale Rise ME16 15 G3
Langham Gro ME16 15 G3
Langton Cl ME14 16 D3
Lansdowne Av ME15 23 E4
Lapins La ME19 12 C4
Larch Cl ME20 7 H3
Larkfield Cl ME20 7 H3
Larkfield Rd ME20 7 H3
Larkfield Trading Est ME20 8 A1
Larking Dr ME16 9 H6
Larkspur Cl ME19 7 G4
Larkspur Rd ME19 7 G4
Larkstore Pk TN12 33 B1
Launder Way ME15 15 H6
Laurel Gro ME17 31 B1
Lavender Cl ME19 7 G4
Lavender Rd ME19 7 G5
Lavender Walk ME19 7 G4
Lavenders Rd ME19 6 D6
Laverstoke Rd ME16 9 G6
Lawrence Cl ME15 22 B2
Laxton Cl ME15 17 G5
Laxton Dr ME17 29 H3
Laxton Walk ME19 12 D3
Leamington Dr ME16 15 F3
Lee Rd ME6 4 B2
Leeds Rd ME17 24 D6
Lees Rd ME18 26 B3
Leicester Rd ME15 23 F2
Leigh Av ME15 22 C3
Len Valley Walk ME15 17 H6
Leney Rd ME18 13 C2
Lenfield Av ME14 16 D3
Lenham Ct ME15 3 F3
Lenham Rd, Ashford TN27 29 F4
Lenham Rd, Maidstone ME17 31 C2
Lenham Storagt Freightflow Depot ME17 32 B6
Lenmead ME17 32 A2
Lenside Dr ME15 17 H6
Leonard Cl ME16 15 F2
Lesley Pl ME16 3 A1
Lested La ME17 30 A2
Lewis Court Dr ME17 28 D1
Lewis Mews ME6 4 B4
Leybourne Way ME20 4 A6
Liberty Sq ME19 12 D3
Libya Ter ME14 16 B1
Lidsing Rd ME14 10 D1
Lilac Grn ME19 7 G4
Lilk Hill ME14 18 A5
Lillieburn ME19 7 E3
Lime Cl TN12 26 B5
Lime Cres ME19 7 G5
Lime Tree Ter ME17 32 D4
Lime Trees TN12 33 B2
Lincoln Rd ME15 23 E2
Linden Rd ME17 21 F6
Lindisfarne Gdns ME16 16 A5
Lindridge La TN12 33 A1
Linkway ME20 8 A5
Linton Gore ME17 27 C1
Linton Hill ME17 28 A4
Linton Rd ME15 22 B6
Liphook Way ME16 9 G5
Lismore Cl ME15 22 B3
Lister Cl ME19 7 F5
Little Buckland Av ME16 15 H2
Little Ct ME16 15 H5
Little Fld TN12 33 B2
Little Market Row ME19 7 E3
Little Orch ME17 27 D1
Little Oxley ME19 7 F2

Littlebourne Rd ME14 17 E1
Livesey St ME18 13 E1
Livingstone Walk ME15 23 G5
Lock La ME16 9 H5
Lockham Farm Av ME15 23 E5
Lockswood ME16 15 H1
Loddington La ME17 28 C5
Loder Cl ME17 32 B5
Lodge Cl ME18 13 B1
Lodge Rd,
  Maidstone ME14 17 F2
Lodge Rd,
  Tonbridge TN12 33 B1
Lombardy Dr ME14 17 E3
London Rd,
  Addington ME19 5 A4
London Rd,
  Aylesford ME20 8 A4
London Rd,
  Leybourne ME19 7 E4
London Rd,
  Maidstone ME16 16 A3
London Rd East ME20 9 E5
Long Rede La ME16 14 D5
Longfield Pl ME15 22 D2
Longfields Dr ME14 17 H3
Longham Copse ME15 23 G1
Longparish Cl ME15 23 G3
Longshaw Rd ME15 23 G5
Longsole Cotts ME16 14 D5
Loose Rd ME16 16 C5
Lord Romneys Hill ME14 17 F4
Love La ME18 13 B2
Lower Bell La ME20 8 A3
Lower Boxley Rd ME14 3 C1
Lower Fant Rd ME16 15 H5
Lower Farm Rd ME17 28 C6
Lower Rd,
  Maidstone ME15 16 C5
Lower Rd,
  Sutton Valence ME17 30 D5
Lower Rd,
  West Farleigh ME15 20 A4
Lower St ME17 25 F3
Lower Stone St ME15 3 D4
Lower Tovil ME15 16 A6
Lubbock Cl ME16 23 G4
Lucas Rd ME6 4 A3
Lucerne St ME14 3 D1
Lucks Hill ME19 6 D5
Lucks Way TN12 26 A5
Luddenham Cl ME14 17 E2
Lughorse La ME18 26 C1
Lullingstone Rd ME16 9 G6
Lundy Cl ME15 22 B3
Lunsford La ME20 7 F1
Lushington Rd ME14 10 A6
Lyle Ct ME16 15 F3
Lymington Ct ME15 23 G5
Lyndhurst Rd ME15 22 D1
Lyngs ME18 26 C3
Lysander Rd ME19 12 B3

Macaulay Cl ME20 7 G1
Mace Ct ME17 27 C1
Madgingford Cl ME15 17 H5
Madgingford Rd ME15 17 G5
Magpie Cl ME20 7 G3
Maidstone
  Ind Centre ME16 3 A2
Maidstone Rd,
  Ashford TN27 29 E4
Maidstone Rd,
  Lenham ME17 32 C5
Maidstone Rd,
  Nettlestead ME18 13 A4
Maidstone Rd,
  Tonbridge TN12 26 B5
Mairs Nest ME19 6 C5
Malden Dr ME14 10 B5
Mallard Walk ME20 7 F3
Mallard Way ME15 17 H6
Malling Rd,
  Kings Hill ME18,19 12 B4
Malling Rd,
  Maidstone ME18 13 E1
Malling Rd,
  Snodland ME6 4 B5
Malling Ter ME16 15 G3
Mallings Dr ME14 18 B3
Mallings La ME14 18 B3
Malta Ter ME14 16 B1
Malthouse Cl ME17 32 C6
Malthouse Hill ME15 22 B5

Mamignot Cl ME14 17 H3
Mandeville Ct ME14 3 E2
Mangravet Av ME15 22 D3
Manor Cl ME14 18 A4
Manor Ct ME14 18 A4
Manor Flds ME15 23 E1
Manor House Dr ME16 15 H4
Manor Rise ME14 18 A4
Mansfield Walk ME16 15 H5
Maple Av ME16 15 G2
Maple Cl ME20 7 H3
Maplesden Cl ME16 14 D5
Marden Rd TN12 33 A2
Marian Sq TN12 33 C3
Marigold Way ME16 15 E5
Marion Cres ME15 22 D1
Market Bldgs ME14 3 C3
Market St TN12 33 C1
Marlborough Par
  ME16 14 D5
Marley Rd ME17 32 C1
Marley Works ME17 32 A4
Marlfield TN12 33 B2
Marlowe Rd ME20 7 G1
Marsh Way ME20 7 H1
Marsham Cl ME14 32 C2
Marsham Cres ME17 30 A3
Marsham St ME14 3 D3
Marston Dr ME14 16 D3
Martin Sq ME20 7 G3
Mary Dukes Pl ME15 3 E4
Mary Last Cl ME6 4 A4
Maryland Dr ME16 14 D6
Masefield Way ME20 7 G1
Matfield Cres ME14 16 D2
Matterdale Gdns ME14 14 C6
Maxton Cl ME14 17 G3
Maxwell Dr ME16 15 F2
May St ME6 4 D2
Mayfair Av ME15 22 C1
Maynards TN12 26 B5
Maypole Dr ME19 12 E3
McAlpine Cres ME15 28 A1
McCabe Cl TN12 33 B4
McKenzie Cl ME20 8 D5
Meades Way TN12 26 A5
Meadow Bank ME19 6 D4
Meadow Bank Mews
  ME19 6 D4
Meadow View Rd ME17 28 D1
Meadow Walk,
  Maidstone ME15 16 C4
Meadow Walk,
  Snodland ME6 4 B3
Meadow Way TN12 26 C5
Meadowdown ME14 17 G3
Medina Rd ME14 8 A4
Medway Av ME18 26 C1
Medway St ME20 9 E3
Medway St ME14 3 B3
**Medway Trading Est
  ME16 16 A5**
Melford Dr ME16 15 F3
Melrose Av ME19 12 E3
Melrose Cl ME15 22 C2
Melville Rd ME15 3 E4
Mercer Cl ME20 7 H1
Mercer Dr ME17 32 D1
Mercer Way ME17 30 A3
Mercers Pl ME19 12 D4
Merchant Pl TN12 26 B5
Merlin Av ME20 7 G3
Merton Rd ME15 15 G3
Meteor Rd ME19 12 C3
**Mid Kent Bsns
Centre ME6 4 C4**
**Mid Kent Shopping
Centre ME16 15 G1**
Middle Mill Rd ME16 7 F5
Middle Row ME14 3 C3
Middlesex Rd ME15 23 E3
Midhurst Ct ME15 3 E4
Midley Cl ME16 14 D5
Midsummer Rd ME6 4 A2
Milford Cl ME15 15 G3
Mill Cl ME17 32 C6
Mill Hall ME20 8 B3
Mill Hall Rd,
  Aylesford ME20 8 A1
Mill Hall Rd,
  Aylesford ME20 8 A3
Mill La, Coxheath ME17 21 G6
Mill La, Maidstone ME14 16 A2

Mill La, Snodland ME6 4 D2
Mill La,
  Wateringbury ME18 13 B1
Mill La, Yalding ME18 26 D3
Mill St, Loose ME15 22 A5
Mill St, Maidstone ME15 3 C3
Mill St, Snodland ME6 4 D2
Mill St,
  West Malling ME19 7 F6
Mill Walk ME16 15 E5
Mill Yd ME19 6 C5
Millbank TN27 29 E4
Millbrook ME19 7 E3
Millbrook ME15 16 A6
Millers Wharf ME15 15 H5
Mills Rd ME20 8 C6
Millstead Cl ME14 16 D3
Milners ME17 25 E4
Milstock Ter ME15 16 A6
Milton Cl ME14 12 D3
Milton La ME19 12 D3
Milton St ME16 15 G6
Mitchell Cl ME17 32 C5
Mitchell Rd ME19 12 C4
Moat Rd TN27 29 E5
Monach Ter ME19 12 E3
Moncktons Av ME14 16 A1
Moncktons Dr ME14 16 A1
Moncktons La ME14 16 A1
Moncrif Cl ME14 18 A3
Monkdown ME15 23 H1
Montfort Dr ME19 12 D4
Montpelier Gate ME16 15 F2
Morella Walk ME17 32 B5
Morhen Cl ME6 4 A4
Morris Cl,
  Maidstone ME15 23 F4
Morris Cl,
  West Malling ME19 7 F4
Morry La ME17 31 B3
Morton Cl ME15 23 E3
Mosquito Rd ME19 12 B3
Mostyn Rd ME14 16 D3
Mote Av ME15 3 F4
Mote Rd ME15 3 E4
Mount Av ME18 26 D2
Mount Dr ME14 18 B4
Mount La ME14 18 A4
Mount Pleasant ME20 9 E3
Mount Pleasant Dr
  ME14
Mountsfield Cl ME16 15 H2
Muir Rd ME16 16 C5
Murrain Dr ME15 23 H1
Museum Av ME14 3 C2
Musket La ME17 19 C5
Mustang Rd ME19 12 C3
Mynn Cres ME14 17 H3

Napier Ct ME14 16 B1
Napoleon Dr TN12 26 B5
Napoleon Walk ME17 32 B5
Neath Ct ME15 23 F2
Nestor Ct ME18 13 E1
Netley Ct ME14 17 E1
Nevill Ct ME19 6 D4
Nevill Pl ME6 4 C4
Nevill Rd ME6 4 C4
Neville Cl ME14 10 C6
New Barns Rd ME14 10 C6
New Cut ME15 21 G3
New Cut Rd ME14 17 E4
New House La TN27 29 E6
New Hythe La,
  Larkfield ME20 7 H3
New Hythe ME20 4 D6
New Lain ME17 32 D6
New Rd, Ashford TN27 29 G5
New Rd, Aylesford ME20 8 A5
New Rd, Langley ME17 24 B4
New Rd,
  Maidstone ME15 23 E2
New Rd,
  West Malling ME19 7 G4
**New Rd Bsns Est
ME20 8 A5**
Newbury Av ME15 15 G1
Newchurch Rd ME15 22 B1
Newenden Cl ME17 17 E1
Newington Walk ME14 17 E1
Newlyn Ct ME15 3 E2
Newlyn Dr TN12 33 C1
Newton Cl ME16 15 H5

Niagara Cl ME19 12 D3
Nicholas Cl ME16 15 E5
Nightingale Cl ME20 7 F3
Norfolk Rd ME15 23 E2
Norman Cl ME14 16 D1
Norman Rd,
  Snodland ME6 4 C4
Norman Rd,
  West Malling ME19 6 B4
Norrington Rd ME15 22 C4
North Cres ME17 21 G6
North Ct ME15 16 C6
North Down TN12 33 B2
North Folly Rd ME15 20 D6
North Mdw ME19 5 C5
North Pole Rd ME16 14 A6
North St, Ashford TN27 29 F5
North St,
  Barming Heath ME16 14 D5
North St,
  Sutton Valence ME17 30 D4
North Vw ME15 22 C1
North Way ME14 10 C6
Northdown Cl ME14 16 C1
Northdowns Vw
  ME17 32 D1
Northfields ME16 14 D5
Northfleet Cl ME14 17 E2
Northleigh Cl ME15 22 C4
Northumberland Ct
  ME15 23 E2
Northumberland Rd
  ME15 23 E2
Norton Rd ME17 30 B3
Norway Ter ME14 16 B1
Nottingham Av ME15 23 F2
Nursery Av,
  Bearsted ME14 18 A4
Nursery Av,
  Maidstone ME16 15 F1
Nursery Rd ME20 8 B5
Nuttall Cl ME14 17 G4

Oak Dr ME20 7 H3
Oak Farm Gdns TN27 29 F4
Oak Gro ME16 15 G2
Oak La TN27 29 G5
Oak Tree Cl TN12 26 C5
Oakapple La ME16 15 E4
Oakfields TN27 29 F4
Oaklands ME15 22 C2
Oaktree Av ME15 23 E3
Oakwood Cl ME16 15 H4
Oakwood Rd ME16 15 G5
Oast Cl ME15 28 C2
Odiham Dr ME16 15 G1
Offens Dr TN12 33 B3
Offham Rd ME19 6 A6
Old Ashford Rd ME17 32 D6
Old Barn Rd ME19 7 E3
Old Chatham Rd,
  Maidstone ME14 10 A1
Old Chatham Rd,
  Sandling ME14 10 A4
Old Dr ME15 22 B3
Old Ham La ME17 32 A6
Old Loose Cl ME15 22 B5
Old Loose Hill ME15 22 B6
Old Mill La ME17 9 G2
Old Mill Rd ME17 25 E2
Old Orchard La ME19 7 E3
Old Parsonage Ct ME19 6 C5
Old Rd ME18 13 A2
Old Ryarsh La ME19 6 B4
Old School La ME17 32 C6
Old School La ME14 6 A1
Old School Pl ME14 3 E2
Old Tovil Rd ME15 16 B6
Old Trafford Cl ME16 15 F1
Old Tree La ME17 23 E6
Old Vinters Rd ME14 3 F2
Oldfield Cl ME15 23 F1
Oliver Rd TN12 33 B3
Orache Dr ME14 17 F2
Orchard Av ME20 8 C4
Orchard Bank ME17 30 A3
**Orchard Bsns Centre
ME16 9 G6**
Orchard Cl,
  Coxheath ME17 21 G6
Orchard Cl,
  Langley ME17 24 D6
Orchard Cl,
  Maidstone ME15 16 C5

Orchard Cres ME18 13 B3
Orchard Dr ME14 17 F4
Orchard Glade TN27 29 G5
Orchard Gro ME20 8 A4
**Orchard Ind Est
ME15 23 H6**
Orchard Pl ME16 16 A4
Orchard St ME15 16 C5
Orchard Vw ME14 11 H5
Orchard Way ME6 4 B3
Oriole Way ME17 7 G2
Orwell Cl ME20 7 F1
Orwell Spike ME19 12 D1
Osbourne Dr ME14 19 D2
Oslin Walk ME14 12 F3
Osprey Walk ME20 7 G3
Ostlers Ct ME6 4 C2
Otham La ME15 18 B6
Otham St ME15 18 B6
Otterbourne Pl ME15 23 G1
Otteridge Rd ME14 18 A4
Owen Cl ME19 7 F4
Owletts Cl ME15 23 E2
Oxford Rd ME15 23 F2
Oxford St ME6 4 C3
Oxley Shaw La ME19 7 E2

Paddlesworth Rd ME6 4 A2
Padsole La ME15 3 E4
Palace Av ME15 3 C4
Palace Ind Est ME15 23 G6
Palmar Rd ME16 15 H2
Palmers Yd TN27 29 C5
Papyrus Way ME20 8 A1
Park Av, Linton ME17 28 A2
Park Av,
  Maidstone ME15 16 C2
Park Barn Rd ME17 25 G5
Park La, Boughton
  Monchelsea ME17 29 E2
Park La,
  Sandling ME14 10 B6
Park Rd,
  Addington ME19 5 B2
Park Rd,
  Leybourne ME19 6 D1
Park View Ct ME15 23 F1
Park Villas ME14 17 F4
Park Way,
  Coxheath ME17 27 C1
Park Way,
  Maidstone ME15 16 C6
**Park Wood
Trading Est ME15 23 H5**
Parkwood Par ME15 23 G5
Partridge Av ME20 7 F2
Passmore Way ME15 22 A1
Pattenden La TN12 26 A4
Paynes La ME15 22 C3
Peacock Mws ME16 3 A3
Pear Tree Av ME20 8 B5
Pear Tree La ME15 22 C4
Pearl Way ME19 12 F3
Peel St ME14 16 B2
Peens La ME17 28 D4
Pelican Ct ME18 13 C2
Pembroke Rd ME17 27 B1
Pembury Gdns ME16 15 H4
Penenden Heath Rd
  ME14 10 D6
Penenden St ME14 16 B2
Penfold Cl ME15 23 F4
Penfold Hill ME17 25 G2
Penfold Way ME15 22 B4
Penhurst Cl ME14 17 G3
Pennine Way ME15 17 H6
Penny Cress Gdns
  ME16 15 G5
Pepingstraw Cl ME19 5 C5
Pepper Alley ME14 10 A6
Perch Cl ME20 4 C6
Peregrine Rd ME19 12 C4
Peridot Ct ME15 23 F5
Perimeter Rd ME20 8 A2
Perry St ME14 16 B2
Perryfield St ME14 16 B2
Pested Bars Rd ME17 23 H4
Pevensey Ct ME16 3 A2
Peverel Dr ME14 17 H3
Pheasant La ME15 22 B3
Phoenix Dr ME18 13 C2
Phoenix Pk ME15 23 G5
Pickering St ME15 22 C4
Pike Cl ME20 4 C6

Pile La TN12 33 D2
Pilgrims Lakes ME17 32 C1
Pilgrims Vw ME14 10 A2
Pilgrims Way ME14 10 C1
Pilgrims Way ME17 32 B5
Pimpernel Cl ME14 18 A3
Pine Cl ME20 7 H3
Pine Gro ME14 16 C1
Pine Lodge ME16 15 G5
Pine Pl ME15 15 H6
Pinnock La TN12 33 A5
Pippin Cl ME17 27 B1
Pippin Way ME19 12 C4
Pitt Rd ME16 15 F6
Plain Rd TN12 26 B6
Plains Av ME15 23 E1
Plaistow Sq ME14 17 E1
Plantation La, Maidstone ME14 17 H4
Plantation La, Tonbridge TN12 26 A5
Pleasant Valley ME15 21 F5
Pleasure House Rd ME17 31 A4
Plough-Wents Rd ME17 29 H2
Plover Rd ME20 7 F3
Plowenders Cl ME19 5 C2
Plumpton Walk ME15 23 G4
Plumtrees ME16 15 E5
Police Station Rd ME19 6 D5
Pope Dr TN12 33 B3
Pope St ME16 15 G5
Popes Wood ME14 17 H2
Poplar Gro ME16 15 F3
Poppy Cl ME16 15 H5
Porchester Cl ME15 22 C3
Port Cl ME14 17 H2
Porters Walk ME17 24 D6
Portland Pl ME6 4 C2
Portsdown Cl ME16 15 F6
Postley Rd ME15 16 C6
Postmill Dr ME15 16 A6
Pout Rd ME6 4 B4
Powell Cl ME20 9 E3
Poyntell Rd TN12 33 C3
Pratling St ME20 9 F2
Premier Par ME20 8 C4
Pridmore Rd ME6 4 B2
Priestley Dr ME20 7 G1
Primrose Dr ME20 8 B5
Princes St ME14 3 E1
Princes Way ME14 19 B3
Priors Dean Cl ME16 14 C6
Priory Cl ME15 21 F2
Priory Gate ME14 3 D2
Priory Gro ME20 8 B4
Priory Rd ME15 16 B4
Progress Est ME15 23 H5
Prospect Pl ME16 16 A5
Provender Way ME14 17 F3
Pudding La ME14 3 C3
Pump Cl ME19 6 D3

Quarry Rd ME15 16 B6
Quarry Sq ME14 16 C2
Quarry Wood Ind Est ME20 8 D6
Queen Anne Rd ME14 3 E3
Queen Elizabeth Sq ME15 23 E3
Queen St ME19 12 D3
Queens Av, Maidstone ME16 15 H2
Queens Av, Snodland ME6 4 C2
Queens Ho ME16 15 E4
Queens Rd, Maidstone ME16 15 F4
Queens Rd, Snodland ME6 4 C2
Queensway ME14 19 B3
Quested Way ME17 32 A2

Radnor Cl ME14 16 A1
Raggatt Pl ME15 16 D6
Ragstone Ct ME20 8 A6
Ragstone Rd ME15 17 H5
Rainham Cl ME15 22 B1
Rampion Cl ME14 17 F2
Randall St ME14 16 B2
Randalls Row ME15 22 A5
Raven Cl ME20 7 G3
Ravens Dane Cl ME15 17 H6
Rawdon Rd ME15 16 C5
Rayfield Ct ME6 4 C2
Rayleigh Cl ME16 9 H6
Raymer Rd ME14 10 C5
Readers Ct ME18 13 E1
Recreation Av ME6 4 B3
Recreation Cl ME14 16 C2
Rectory Cl ME6 4 C3
Rectory La, Harrietsham ME17 32 C2
Rectory La, Maidstone ME16 21 E1
Rectory La, Sutton Valence ME17 30 D5
Rectory La North ME19 7 E2
Rectory La South ME19 7 F3
Reculver Walk ME15 23 G2
Red Hill ME18 13 C1
Red House Gdns ME18 13 B1
Redbank ME19 7 F3
Redcliffe La ME14 16 C1
Rede Wood Rd ME16 14 C4
Redsells Cl ME15 17 H6
Redwall La ME17 27 A4
Redwell Gro ME19 12 F4
Redwing Cl ME20 7 G2
Reed Cl ME20 4 C6
Reeves Cl TN12 33 B2
Reeves Ct ME19 7 H4
Regent Dr ME15 22 C2
Regent Way ME19 12 F3
Reginald Rd ME16 16 A5
Reinden Gro ME15 17 G6
Restharrow Rd ME14 17 F3
Rhodewood Cl ME15 23 H1
Richmond Way ME15 22 B2
Ridgway ME16 15 F6
Ringlestone Cres ME14 10 A5
Ringwood Rd ME15 22 D1
Ritch Rd ME6 4 A3
River Bank Cl ME15 3 F3
River Cl ME15 21 E2
River Vw ME15 16 B5
River Way ME20 7 H1
Riverhead Cl ME16 15 G2
Rivers Cl ME18 13 C2
Rivers Walk ME17 32 B5
Roberts Orchard Rd ME16 14 D5
Roberts Rd ME6 4 B2
Robins Av ME17 32 B6
Robins Cl ME17 32 B6
Robson Dr ME20 8 B4
Rocfort Rd ME6 4 C3
Rochester Rd ME20 9 E3
Rock Rd ME14 16 C1
Rockwell Ct ME15 22 A1
Rocky Hill ME16 3 A4
Rocky Hill Ter ME16 3 A4
Roman Heights ME14 16 D1
Roman Rd ME6 4 B2
Romney Cl ME15 17 H5
Romney Pl ME15 3 D4
Rookery Hill ME6 4 B3
Rose Ter ME19 5 C5
Rose Yd ME14 3 C3
Roseacre Gdns ME14 18 A4
Roseacre La ME14 17 H4
Roseholme ME16 15 H5
Roseleigh Av ME16 15 G3
Rosemary Rd, Maidstone ME15 17 H5
Rosemary Rd, West Malling ME19 7 G4
Rosemead Gdns TN27 29 E4
Rosemount Cl ME15 22 B6
Rosslyn Grn ME16 15 F2
Rougemont ME19 12 E3
Roughetts Rd ME19 5 D1
Roundel Way TN12 26 B5
Roundhay ME19 7 E4
Roundwell ME14 18 C4
Rowan Cl ME20 8 C4
Rowland Cl ME16 16 A4
Royal British Legion Industries ME20 8 D4
Royal Engineers Rd ME14 10 A5
Royal Star Arc ME14 3 C3
Royston Rd ME15 17 H5
Royton Av ME17 32 C5
Rubin Pl ME19 12 E3
Runnymede Gdns ME15 22 C2
Rushford Cl TN27 29 F5
Rushmead Dr ME15 22 C3
Ruskin Cl ME19 7 F4
Russet Ct ME17 27 C1
Russett Cl ME20 8 C5
Russett Way ME19 12 C4
Rutland Way ME15 23 F1
Ryan Dr ME15 17 H6
Ryarsh La ME19 6 C4
Rycault Cl ME16 16 A4

Saddlers Cl ME14 17 G2
Saffron Cl ME16 15 F5
Sage Ct ME16 15 E4
St Andrews Cl ME16 15 E5
St Andrews Rd ME16 15 E5
St Annes Ct ME16 3 A3
St Barnabas Cl ME16 9 G6
St Benedict Rd ME6 4 A3
St Davids Gate ME16 15 E5
St Faiths La ME14 18 A4
St Faiths St ME14 3 B2
St Francis Cl ME14 16 D1
St Georges Sq ME16 15 H4
St Helens La ME15 20 C2
St Heliers Cl ME16 15 F5
St James Cl ME19 7 G5
St Katherines La ME6 4 B3
St Laurence Av ME16 9 F6
St Leonards Rd ME16 9 G5
St Leonards St ME19 6 B6
St Lukes Av ME14 3 F1
St Lukes Rd ME14 3 F1
St Margarets Cl ME16 15 F5
St Martins Cl ME14 11 H5
St Marys Ct ME19 6 B5
St Michaels Cl ME20 9 F3
St Michaels Rd ME16 15 H5
St Peter St ME16 3 A2
St Peters Bri ME16 3 B4
St Peters Cl ME20 8 A5
St Peters Rd ME20 8 A5
St Phillips Av ME15 16 C5
St Ronans Cl ME15 22 D3
St Saviours Rd ME15 23 F3
St Stephen Sq ME15 16 A6
St Vincents La ME19 5 A3
St Welcumes Way ME17 32 C2
Salem St ME15 16 C5
Salisbury Rd ME14 16 C1
Salters Cross ME18 26 D2
Saltings Rd ME6 4 C4
Salts Av ME15 28 B1
Salts La ME15 22 B5
Saltwood Rd ME15 16 B6
Samphire Cl ME14 17 F3
Sandbourne Dr ME14 10 B5
Sandling La ME14 10 A4
Sandling Rd ME14 3 C1
Sandown Rd ME19 6 B5
Sandway Rd ME17 32 C3
Sandy La, Bearsted ME14 18 A3
Sandy La, Maidstone ME14 10 D6
Sandy La, Snodland ME6 4 A4
Sandy La, West Malling ME19 6 A4
Sandy Mt ME14 18 A3
Sasoon Cl ME20 7 G1
Saxon Cl ME19 12 C4
Saxons Dr ME14 16 D1
School La, Maidstone ME15 23 F1
School La, Sutton Valence ME17 30 D5
School La, Tonbridge TN12 33 C3
Scotney Gdns ME16 3 B2
Scott Cl ME20 8 A5
Scott St ME14 16 B2
Scragged Oak Rd ME14 19 C2
Scrubbs La ME16 15 H3
Sedley Cl ME20 8 D4
Selbourne Walk ME15 23 G4
Selby Rd ME15 23 G5
Senacre La ME15 23 G4
Senacre Sq ME15 23 G3
Sessions House Sq ME14 3 C1
Sevington Pk ME15 22 B3
Shaftesbury Cl ME19 7 F4
Shaftesbury Dr ME16 15 G3
Sharnal La ME6 4 C4
Sharps Fld TN27 29 G5
Sharsted Way ME14 18 A2
Shaw Cl ME14 11 E6
Sheals Cres ME15 16 C6
Shearers Cl ME14 17 F3
Shearwater ME16 15 F3
Sheldon Way ME20 7 H2
Shelley Rd ME16 15 G6
Shenley Gro ME14 10 A3
Shepherds Gate Dr ME14 17 F2
Shepherds Way ME17 24 D6
Sheppey Rd ME15 22 B3
Shepway Ct ME15 23 E2
Sherbourne Dr ME16 15 F6
Sheridan Cl ME14 10 A6
Sheringham Cl ME16 9 H6
Shernolds ME15 22 C2
Sherway Cl TN27 29 H5
Shilingheld Cl ME14 17 G2
Shingle Barn La ME15 20 A6
Shipley Ct ME14 3 D2
Shirley Way ME15 17 H5
Shoreham Walk ME15 23 G3
Shortlands Grn ME15 23 G4
Shropshire Ter ME15 23 F2
Shrubsole Dr ME14 10 A3
Sidney St ME16 15 G6
Silchester Ct ME14 10 D6
Silverdale ME16 15 E5
Simmonds La ME15 24 A3
Simpson Rd ME6 4 B4
Siskin Walk ME20 7 G2
Sissinghurst Dr ME16 15 F3
Sittingbourne Rd, Detling ME14 11 F6
Sittingbourne Rd, Maidstone ME14 3 F2
Skinners Way ME17 24 D6
Skye Cl ME15 22 C3
Slaney Rd TN12 33 C3
Small Hythe Cl ME15 18 A5
Small Profits ME18 13 D4
Smarden Rd TN27 29 H5
Smiths Hill ME15 20 A6
Snodland By-Pass ME6 4 B5
Snodland Rd ME6 4 A4
Snowdon Av ME14 3 F2
Snowdon Par ME14 16 D3
Somerfield Cl ME16 15 H3
Somerfield La ME16 15 H3
Somerfield Rd ME16 15 H3
Somerset Rd ME15 22 D2
Somner Walk ME15 23 G6
Sort Mill Rd ME6 4 D3
South Bank, Maidstone ME17 30 D5
South Bank, Tonbridge TN12 33 B4
South Cres ME17 21 G6
South Ct ME15 22 C1
South La ME17 30 D6
South Park ME15 22 C1
South Park Rd ME15 16 D6
South Rd TN12 26 C5
South St ME16 14 D6
Southaylesford Retail Pk ME20 8 C5
Southey Way ME20 7 G1
Southways ME17 30 C4
Southwood ME16 14 D5
Sovereigns Way TN12 26 A5
Spearhead Rd ME14 10 B6
Spectrum Bsns Centre ME15 23 G5
Spectrum West ME16 9 H5
Speedwell Cl ME14 17 F3
Speldhurst Ct ME16 15 G3
Spencer Way ME15 23 G2
Spindle Glade ME14 17 E2
Spitfire Rd ME19 12 B3
Spot La ME15 17 H6
Springett Way ME17 21 H6
Springfield Av ME14 16 A1
Springfield Quays ME14 16 A1
Springfield Rd ME20 7 F1
Springvale ME16 3 A3
Springwood Cl ME16 15 E5
Springwood Rd ME16 15 E4
Spruce Cl ME20 7 H3
Spurway ME14 17 H4
Square Hill ME15 3 F3
Square Hill Rd ME15 3 F4
Staceys St ME14 3 B1
Stadler Cl ME16 15 H1
Staffa Rd ME15 22 B3
Stagshaw Cl ME15 16 C6
Stanford Dr ME16 15 G5
Stanhope Cl ME14 10 A6
Stanley Cl TN12 33 B3
Stanley Rd TN12 26 C5
Stansted Cl ME16 15 G1
Staple Dr TN12 33 C3
Staplers Ct ME14 10 D6
Starnes Ct ME14 3 D2
Station App, Ashford TN27 29 G5
Station App, Maidstone ME16 3 B4
Station App, Tonbridge TN12 33 B1
Station Hill ME15 21 E2
Station Rd, Ashford TN27 29 F5
Station Rd, Aylesford ME20 8 A4
Station Rd, Harrietsham ME17 32 B1
Station Rd, Lenham ME17 32 B6
Station Rd, Maidstone ME14 3 C1
Station Rd, Tonbridge TN12 33 B1
Stede Hill ME17 32 C1
Stella Cl TN12 26 B5
Sterling Av ME16 15 G3
Sterry Gdns ME15 23 F2
Stevens Cl ME6 4 C2
Stevenson Cl ME15 16 B5
Stevenson Way ME20 7 F1
Stickens La ME19 7 F6
Stile Bridge La ME17 28 C6
Stirling Rd ME19 12 C3
Stockbury Dr ME16 15 H1
Stockett La ME17 21 G6
Stockton Cl ME14 10 D6
Stoneacre Ct ME15 22 C1
Stoneacre La ME15 24 A2
Straford Dr ME15 23 E4
Stratford Rd ME19 6 B5
Straw Mill Hill ME15 16 A6
Streamside ME20 8 A4
Stuart Cl ME14 16 D1
Sturmer Ct ME19 12 C4
Styles La ME14 11 E2
Suffolk Rd ME15 23 E1
Sunburst Cl TN12 26 B5
Sunningdale Ct ME15 3 F3
Sunrise Way ME19 12 F3
Super Abbey Est ME20 9 F3
Surrenden Rd TN12 33 B3
Surrey Rd ME15 23 E1
Sussex Rd ME15 23 E1
Sutton Ct TN12 26 B5
Sutton Forge TN12 26 B5
Sutton Rd ME15 22 D1
Sutton St ME14 18 C4
Sutton Valence Hill ME17 30 D5
Swadelands Cl ME17 32 C5
Swallow Rd ME20 7 F3
Swan St ME19 6 C4
Sweet Briar Ct ME16 15 H2
Sweetlands La TN12 33 D2
Swift Cl ME20 7 G2
Sycamore Cres ME16 15 G2
Sycamore Dr ME20 8 C5

Talbot Rd ME16 15 G1
Tall Trees Cl ME17 31 B1
Target Bsns Centre ME15 23 H6
Tarragon Rd ME16 15 E4
Tasker Cl ME15 18 A5
Tassel Cl ME19 7 G4
Tattershall Rd ME15 22 C1
Taunton Cl ME15 23 H4
Taylor Cl ME17 32 B2
Taylor Rd ME6 4 B3
Teapot La ME20 8 C5
Teasaucer Hill ME15 22 B2
Teasel Cl ME14 17 G3
Tempest Rd ME19 12 C3
Temple Way ME19 7 F4
Terminus Rd ME16 15 E5

Terrace Rd ME16 3 A4
Terry Walk ME19 7 F2
Teston La ME18 13 F2
Teston Rd,
 Offham ME19 5 A5
Teston Rd,
 West Malling ME19 12 D1
Thackeray Rd ME20 7 G2
Thatch Barn Rd TN27 29 G4
Thatcher Rd TN12 33 B2
The Almonds ME14 18 A3
The Avenue ME20 8 C4
The Beacons ME17 27 C1
The Beams ME15 23 G1
The Beeches ME20 8 C4
The Bounds ME20 8 C5
The Brucks ME18 13 C2
The Chapel ME16 15 E4
The Cherries ME16 15 E6
The Chestnuts ME19 5 B2
The Cloisters ME17 32 B5
The Close ME19 5 B2
The Cockpit TN12 26 B5
The Coppice ME20 8 D4
The Crescent ME14 10 B6
The Croft ME19 7 F2
The Dunnings ME16 15 E5
The Ferns ME20 7 H3
The Gardens ME17 21 G6
The Grange ME19 7 G6
The Green,
 Bearsted ME14 18 B3
The Green, Boughton
 Monchelsea ME17 28 D1
The Green,
 East Farleigh ME15 21 F3
The Green,
 West Malling ME19 5 C2
The Grove ME14 17 H4
The Groves ME6 4 B3
The Hampshires ME17 32 A2
The Harbour ME17 30 D6
The Hawthorns ME20 8 C4
The Head Race ME15 15 H6
The Hedgerow ME14 17 G2
The Hedges ME14 10 C6
The Hurstings ME15 15 H5
The Lakes ME20 4 C6
The Landway ME14 17 H4
The Laurels ME16 15 F5
The Laxey ME15 16 A6
The Lindens ME20 8 C4
The Links ME19 5 D3
The Mallows ME14 16 A1
The Maltings,
 Grove Green ME14 17 F2
The Maltings,
 Maidstone ME17 22 D6
The Mead ME19 7 F2
The Meadows ME15 16 A6
The Medlars ME14 17 E2
The Mews,
 Ashford TN27 29 B5
The Mews,
 Maidstone ME16 3 A1
The Mill Hall
 Bsns Est ME20 **8 B3**
The Moorings ME15 16 B5
The Mortocks ME14 16 B2
The Nook ME18 26 C1
The Oaks ME20 8 C4
The Oasts ME14 18 B3
The Old Bailey ME17 32 C2
The Old Oast
 Bsns Centre ME20 **9 E4**
The Orchard ME14 18 A3
The Orpines ME18 13 D2
The Parade TN12 33 C4
The Pavings ME17 19 D6
The Penstocks ME15 15 H6
The Platt ME17 30 D5
The Quarries ME17 22 D6
The Quern ME15 16 A6
The Rocks Rd ME19 14 A3
The Rushes ME20 7 H1
The Russets ME16 15 F3
The Sovereigns ME16 15 H3
The Spillway ME15 15 H6
The Spinney ME15 16 D5
The Spires ME16 15 H3
The Sprig ME14 17 H3
The Square ME17 32 D5
The Stampers ME15 15 H6
The Stream ME20 8 A4
The Street,
 Bearsted ME14 18 B3
The Street, Boxley ME14 11 E2
The Street, Detling ME14 19 B3
The Street, Teston ME18 13 F2
The Street,
 West Malling ME19 6 A1
The Tail Race ME15 15 H6
The Tatt ME18 26 C2
The Thatchers ME16 15 F3
The Topiary ME14 17 H4
The Valley ME17 27 D1
The Waldens ME17 31 C1
The Walk ME17 31 C1
The Weavers ME16 15 F3
The Wheelwrights ME17 32 B2
The Wychlings ME17 31 B2
Thirlmere Cl ME16 9 H6
Thistledown ME14 17 G3
Thomson Cl ME6 4 C2
Thorn Rd TN12 26 C6
Thorneycroft Cl ME17 31 B1
Thornhill Pl ME14 16 B2
Threshers Dr ME14 17 F3
Thurlestone Ct ME14 16 B2
Thurnham La ME14 18 B3
Thyme Walk ME16 15 F5
Tichborne Cl ME16 15 G1
Tilefields ME17 19 D6
Tilghman Way ME6 4 D2
Tintern Rd ME16 15 G1
Titchfield Cl ME15 23 G3
Titchfield Rd ME15 23 G3
Tithe Yd ME17 32 C6
Tollgate Pl TN27 29 G5
Tollgate Way ME14 10 A2
Tom Joyce Cl ME6 4 B4
Tomlin Cl,
 Snodland ME6 4 B2
Tomlin Cl,
 Tonbridge TN12 33 B2
Tonbridge Ct ME16 15 H5
Tonbridge Rd,
 Maidstone ME16 3 A4
Tonbridge Rd,
 Wateringbury ME18 13 A1
Tovil Green
 Bsns Centre ME15 **16 A6**
Tovil Green
 Bsns Pk ME15 **15 H6**
Tovil Grn ME15 15 H6
Tovil Hill ME15 16 A6
Tovil Rd ME15 16 A6
Tower Gdns ME14 18 A4
Tower Hill ME19 5 C6
Tower La ME14 18 A4
Tower Vw ME19 12 E1
Town Hill ME19 6 C4
Town Hill Cl ME19 6 C4
Townsend Rd ME6 4 A2
Townsend Sq ME19 12 D4
Trapfield Cl ME14 18 B4
Trapfield La ME14 18 B4
Trapham Rd ME16 15 H3
Trellyn Cl ME16 14 D6
Trenton Cl ME16 15 F1
Trevor Dr ME16 15 F2
Trewin Cl ME20 8 B4
Trinity Ct ME20 9 E3
Troodos Hill ME14 10 B5
Trottiscliffe Rd ME19 5 B1
Troutbeck Ho ME20 8 A4
Tudor Av ME14 16 D1
Tufton St ME14 3 E2
Tumblers Hill ME17 31 A5
Turgis Cl ME17 24 D6
Turkey Ct ME15 17 E4
Twisden Rd ME19 7 G5
Twyford Ct ME14 17 E2
Tydeman Rd ME15 17 G5
Tyland La ME14 10 A2
Tyler Cl ME19 7 F4
Typhoon Rd ME19 12 C3

Ufton Cl ME15 23 G1
Ulcombe Hill ME17 31 D3
Ulcombe Rd,
 Ashford TN27 29 F4
Ulcombe Rd,
 Maidstone ME17 24 D6
Underwood Cl ME15 16 B5
Unicumes La ME16 15 G6
Union Pk ME15 **23 G6**
Union St ME14 3 D2
Unwin Cl ME20 9 E2
Upper Barnhill ME15 20 C6
Upper Fant Rd ME16 15 G6
Upper Hunton Hill ME15 27 A1
Upper Mill ME18 13 B1
Upper Rd ME15 16 C5
Upper St ME17 25 E5
Upper Stone St ME15 3 D4
Uptons TN27 29 F4
Usborne Cl TN12 33 B4

Vale Rd ME15 22 A5
Valentine Rd ME15 23 G3
Valley Dr ME15 22 B4
Vanity La ME17 27 D3
Vauxhall Cres ME6 4 B5
Veles Rd ME6 4 B3
Vicarage Cl ME20 9 E3
Vicarage La ME15 21 E3
Vicarage Rd ME18 26 C2
Vicary Way ME16 15 H2
Victoria Ct ME16 16 A4
Victoria Dr ME19 12 C4
Victoria La ME14 3 C1
Victoria Orch ME16 15 F4
Victoria Par ME14 3 C1
Victoria St ME16 16 A4
Vine Walk TN12 33 B4
Vinters Rd ME14 3 F2
Vinters Way ME14 17 G3

Wades Cl TN12 26 C5
Waghorn Rd ME6 4 C2
Wagoners Cl ME14 17 F4
Wakehurst Cl ME17 21 F6
Waldron Dr ME15 22 B4
Wallis Av ME15 23 G5
Wallis Av West ME15 23 F4
Walmer Ct ME14 3 D2
Walnut Cl ME18 26 C1
Walnut Tree Av ME15 22 C4
Walnut Tree Ct ME19 7 H4
Walnut Tree La ME15 22 B4
Walpole Cl ME19 7 F4
Warden Cl ME16 15 G3
Warden Mill Cl ME18 13 C2
Wardes ME18 26 C1
Ware St ME14 17 H2
Warmlake Ind Est
 ME17 **30 C3**
Warmlake Rd ME17 30 A3
Warnett Ct ME6 4 C2
Warnford Gdns ME15 22 C2
Warwick Pl ME16 16 A4
Wat Tyler Way ME15 3 E4
Water La,
 Maidstone ME15 3 D3
Water La,
 Thurnham ME14 18 C4
Water La,
 Ulcombe ME17 31 D1
Water La,
 West Malling ME19 6 C5
Waterloo St ME15 16 C5
Waterlow Rd ME14 16 C2
Watermill Cl ME16 15 F3
Waters Edge ME15 16 B5
Waterside ME14 3 B2
Waterside Ct ME19 7 F2
Waterside Gate ME16 3 A1
Waterside Mws ME18 13 C3
Watersmeet Cl ME15 22 B1
Watkins Cl TN12 33 B2
Watts Cl ME6 4 D2
Waverley Cl ME17 27 C1
Wayland ME14 18 A4
Weald Cl ME15 23 E4
Wealden Way ME20 8 C6
Weavering St ME14 17 F4
Weavers Cl TN12 33 C2
Wedgewood Cl ME16 15 F3
Week St ME14 3 C2
Weld Cl TN12 33 C3
Well Rd ME14 3 D1
Well St,
 Maidstone ME15 22 A6
Well St,
 West Malling ME19 7 E6
Wellington Pl ME14 16 B2
Wellington Way ME19 12 C3
Wents Wood ME14 17 G2
Wesley Cl ME16 14 D5
West Ct ME15 22 C1
West Dr ME17 31 C4
West End TN12 26 A5
West Malling Ind Pk
 ME19 **5 D3**
West Mill Rd ME20 8 A2
West Park Rd ME15 16 D5
West St,
 Maidstone ME17 32 A2
West St,
 West Malling ME19 6 C5
West Walk ME16 15 F5
Westerhill Rd ME17 27 C2
Western Rd ME16 15 F5
Westmarsh Cl ME15 23 G2
Westmead ME20 4 D6
Westminster Sq ME16 15 F3
Westmorland Cl ME15 23 F2
Westmorland Grn ME15 23 F2
Westmorland Rd ME15 23 F2
Westree Ct ME16 16 A4
Westree Rd ME16 16 A4
Westway ME17 21 G6
Westwood Rd ME15 22 B2
Weyhill Cl ME14 17 E1
Wharf Rd ME15 16 A5
Wharfedale Sq ME15 16 A6
Whatman Cl ME14 16 D1
Wheatfield ME19 7 E3
Wheatfields ME14 17 F3
Wheatsheaf Cl ME15 22 C2
Wheelbarrow
 Park Est TN12 **26 A4**
Wheeler Pl ME19 12 D4
Wheeler St,
 Ashford TN27 29 G5
Wheeler St,
 Maidstone ME14 3 D2
Wheeler St Hedges
 ME14 16 C2
Wheelers La ME17 27 D4
Whiffen Walk ME19 7 H4
Whimbrel Grn ME20 7 G3
Whitchurch Cl ME16 15 H3
White Horse La ME15 23 H3
White Rock Pl ME16 16 A4
Whitebeam Dr ME17 21 F6
Whitedyke Rd ME6 4 B1
Whitehall Dr ME17 31 B2
Whiteheads La ME14 18 A4
Whitmore St ME16 15 G5
Wickens Pl ME19 6 C5
Wickham Pl ME17 32 D5
Wierton Rd ME17 29 F2
Wilberforce Rd ME17 21 G6
Wildwood Cl ME17 31 C2
Wilkinson Pl ME19 12 D4
Willington Grn ME15 23 F3
Willington St ME15 23 F2
Willow Cres TN12 33 C1
Willow Industries
 ME14 **10 A3**
Willow Mead ME19 7 F2
Willow Rd ME20 7 F2
Willow Rise ME15 17 H6
Willow Way ME15 16 D5
Willowbank Ct ME15 3 F3
Willowside ME6 4 C2
Wilson Cl ME15 23 G2
Wilson Ct ME18 26 C2
Wilsons La ME15 21 E5
Wilton Dr ME20 8 A5
Wiltshire Way ME15 23 F2
Winchs Garth TN12 33 C1
Windmill Ct ME17 28 C1
Windmill Heights ME14 18 A3
Windmill La East ME19 6 C6
Windmill La West ME19 12 D1
Windsor Cl ME14 16 D2
Wingham Cl ME15 23 G3
Wingrove Dr ME14 17 F3
Winifred Rd ME15 17 H5
Winston Av ME19 12 E3
Winterfield La ME19 7 F5
Wodehouse Cl ME20 4 B6
Wolfe Rd ME16 15 F6
Wood Cl ME20 8 C6
Woodbridge Dr ME15 16 A6
Woodcocks TN27 29 F5
Woodcut ME14 10 C5
Woodford Gro ME19 12 E3
Woodford Rd ME16 15 F6
Woodgate Rd ME19 5 B1
Woodland Cl ME19 6 B4
Woodland Way ME14 10 C6
Woodlands ME17 27 B1
Woodlands Av ME6 4 B2
Woodlands Cl,
 Penenden Heath ME14 10 C6
Woodlands Cl,
 Teston ME18 13 F1
Woodlands Par ME20 8 B5
Woodlands Rd ME20 8 A5
Woodlea ME19 7 F3
Woodleas ME16 14 D5
Woodpecker Rd ME20 7 F3
Woodside Rd ME15 22 D3
Woodville Rd ME15 16 C5
Woolaston Cl ME15 16 B6
Wooley Rd ME15 23 G2
Woollett St ME14 3 D1
Worcester Av ME19 12 C4
Worcester Rd ME15 23 F3
Wordsworth Rd ME14 10 D6
Wordsworth Way ME20 7 G1
Workhouse La,
 Coxheath ME15 21 F5
Workhouse La,
 Sutton Valence ME17 31 B4
Worsfold Ct ME15 22 C1
Wotton Cl ME15 23 G4
Wrangleden Cl ME15 23 F5
Wrangleden Rd ME15 23 F4
Wren Cl ME20 7 F3
Wren Ind Est ME15 **23 G6**
Wyatt St ME14 3 E3
Wyke Manor Rd ME14 3 D3
Wykeham Gro ME17 25 F3
Wytherling Cl ME14 17 G3
Wyvern Cl ME6 4 C3

Yalding Hill,
 Maidstone ME18 20 A6
Yalding Hill,
 Yalding ME18 26 C2
Yarrow Ct ME14 17 H3
Yeoman Ct ME14 18 A5
Yeoman La ME14 18 A5
Yeoman Pk ME15 18 A6
Yeoman Way ME15 17 H6
Yew Tree Cl ME20 8 C4
Yew Tree Cotts ME14 10 B4
Yew Tree Ind Est
 ME20 **8 B3**
York Rd ME15 16 D6

Red Books showing the way

For the latest publication list, prices and to order online please visit our website.

LOCAL and SUPER RED BOOKS
(Super Red Books are shown in **Bold** Type)

Abingdon & Didcot
Aldershot & Camberley
Alfreton & Belper
Andover
Ashford & Tenterden
Aylesbury & Tring
Bangor & Caernarfon
Barnstaple & Bideford
Basildon & Billericay
Basingstoke & Andover
Bath & Bradford-upon-Avon
Bedford
Bodmin & Wadebridge
Bournemouth
Bracknell & Wokingham
Brentwood
Brighton
Bristol
Bromley (London Borough)
Burton-upon-Trent & Swadlincote
Bury St. Edmunds & Stowmarket
Cambridge
Cannock & Rugeley
Cardiff
Cardiff City & Bay Visitors Map (Sheet Map)
Carlisle & Penrith
Chelmsford
Chester
Chester & Wrexham
Chesterfield & Dronfield
Chichester & Bognor Regis
Chippenham & Calne
Coatbridge & Airdrie
Colchester & Clacton-on-Sea
Corby & Kettering
Coventry
Crawley & Mid Sussex
Crewe
Derby
Dundee & St. Andrews
Eastbourne
Edinburgh
Exeter & Exmouth
Falkirk & Grangemouth
Fareham & Gosport
Flintshire Towns
Folkestone & Dover
Glasgow
Gloucester & Cheltenham
Gravesend & Dartford
Grays & Thurrock
Great Yarmouth & Lowestoft
Grimsby & Cleethorpes
Guildford & Woking
Hamilton & Motherwell
Harlow & Bishops Stortford
Harrogate & Knaresborough
Hastings & Bexhill
Hereford
Hertford & Waltham Cross
High Wycombe
Huntingdon & St. Neots
Ipswich
Isle of Man
Isle of Wight (Complete Coverage)
Kendal & Windermere
Kidderminster
Kingston upon Hull
Lancaster & Morecambe
Leicester
Lincoln
Llandudno & Colwyn Bay
Loughborough & Coalville
Luton & Dunstable
Macclesfield & Wilmslow
Maidstone
Mansfield
Medway & Gillingham
Mid Wales Towns
Milton Keynes
New Forest Towns
Newbury & Thatcham
Newport & Chepstow
Newquay & Perranporth
Northampton
Northwich & Winsford
Norwich

Nottingham
Nuneaton & Bedworth
Oxford & Kidlington
Penzance & St. Ives
Perth
Peterborough
Plymouth
Portsmouth
Reading & Henley-on-Thames
Redditch & Kidderminster
Reigate & Mole Valley
Rhyl & Prestatyn
Rugby
St. Albans, Welwyn & Hatfield
St. Austell & Lostwithiel
Salisbury & Wilton
Scarborough & Whitby
Scunthorpe
Sevenoaks
Shrewsbury
Sittingbourne & Faversham
Slough, Maidenhead & Windsor
Solihull
Southampton
Southend-on-Sea
Stafford
Stevenage & Letchworth
Stirling & Alloa
Stoke-on-Trent
Stroud & Nailsworth
Swansea
Swindon
Tamworth & Lichfield
Taunton & Bridgwater
Telford & Newport
Tenby & Saundersfoot (Colour)
Thanet & Canterbury
Torbay
Trowbridge & Frome
Truro & Falmouth
Tunbridge Wells & Tonbridge
Walsall
Warwick & Royal Leamington Spa
Watford & Hemel Hempstead
Wellingborough & Rushden
Wells & Glastonbury
West Midlands & Birmingham (Spiral)
Weston-super-Mare
Weymouth & Dorchester
Winchester
Wolverhampton (Sheet Map)
Worcester
Workington & Whitehaven
Worthing & Littlehampton
Wrexham
York

COUNTY RED BOOKS
(Town Centre Maps)

Bedfordshire
Berkshire
Buckinghamshire
Cambridgeshire
Cheshire
Cornwall
Cumbria
Derbyshire
Devon
Dorset
Essex
Gloucestershire
Hampshire
Herefordshire
Hertfordshire
Kent
Leicestershire & Rutland
Lincolnshire
Norfolk
Northamptonshire
Nottinghamshire
Oxfordshire
Shropshire
Somerset
Staffordshire
Suffolk
Surrey
Sussex (East)
Sussex (West)
Warwickshire

Wiltshire
Worcestershire

EUROPEAN STREET MAPS
Calais & Boulogne Shoppers Map (Sheet Map)
Dieppe Shoppers Map (Sheet Map)
North French Towns Street Atlas

OFFICIAL TOURIST MAPS and TOURIST MAPS
(Official Tourist Maps are shown in **Bold** Type)

-	Wales / Cymru Tourist Atlas 1:200,000
-	Kent to Cornwall 1:460,000
1	**South East England** 1:200,000
101	**Kent & East Sussex** 1:150,000
102	**Surrey & Sussex Downs** 1:150,000
103	South East England Leisure Map 1:200,000
104	**Sussex** 1:150,000
2	**Southern England** 1:200,000
201	Isle of Wight 1:50,000
3	**Wessex** 1:200,000
301	Dorset 1:150,000
4	**Devon & Cornwall** 1:200,000
401	**Cornwall** 1:180,000
402	**Devon** 1:200,000
403	**Dartmoor & South Devon Coast** 1:100,000
404	**Exmoor & North Devon** 1:100,000
5	Greater London (M25 Map) 1:80,000
6	**East Anglia** 1:200,000
7	**Chilterns & Thames Valley** 1:200,000
8	**Cotswolds & Severn Valley** 1:200,000
802	The Cotswolds 1:110,000
9	**Wales** 1:250,000
10	**The Shires of Middle England** 1:250,000
11	**The Mid Shires** (Staffs, Shrops, etc.) 1:200,000
111	**Peak District** 1:100,000
12	Snowdonia 1:125,000
13	**Yorkshire** 1:200,000
131	**Yorkshire Dales** 1:125,000
132	**North Yorkshire Moors** 1:125,000
14	**North West England** 1:200,000
141	Isle of Man 1:95,000
15	**North Pennines & Lakes** 1:200,000
151	Lake District 1:75,000
16	**Borders of Scotland & England** 1:200,000
17	**Burns Country** 1:200,000
18	Heart of Scotland 1:200,000
181	**Greater Glasgow** 1:150,000
182	**Edinburgh & The Lothians** 1:150,000
183	**Isle of Arran** 1:63,360
184	**Fife (Kingdom of)** 1:100,000
19	**Loch Lomond** 1:150,000
191	**Argyll, The Isles & Loch Lomond** 1:275,000
20	**Perthshire** 1:150,000
21	**Fort William, Ben Nevis, Glen Coe** 1:185,000
211	Iona and Mull 1:10,000 / 1:115,000
22	**Grampian Highlands** 1:185,000
23	**Loch Ness & Aviemore** 1:150,000
24	**Skye & Lochalsh** 1:130,000
25	**Argyll & The Isles** 1:200,000
26	**Caithness & Sutherland** 1:185,000
27	Outer Hebrides 1:200,000
28	**Orkney Shetland** 1:128,000 } same map
28	**Shetland & Orkney** 1:128,000
30	**Highlands of Scotland** 1:275,000
92	England & Wales 1:650,000
93	Scotland 1:500,000
94	Historic Scotland 1:500,000
95	Scotland (Homelands of the Clans)
99	Great Britain 1:1,100,000
99	Great Britain (Flat) 1:1,100,000
100	British Isles 1:1,100,000

EUROPEAN LEISURE MAPS
Europe 1:3,100,000
Cross Channel Visitors' Map 1:530,000
France 1:1,000,000
Germany 1:1,000,000
Ireland 1:625,000
Italy 1:1,000,000
Netherlands, Belgium & Luxembourg 1:600,000
Spain & Portugal 1:1,000,000

WORLD MAPS
World Map - Political (Folded) 1:29,000,000
World Map - Political (Flat in Tube) 1:29,000,000
World Travel Adventure Map (Folded) 1:29,000,000
World Travel Adventure Map (Flat in Tube) 1:29,000,000

RED BOOKS (ESTATE PUBLICATIONS) Ltd, Bridewell House, Tenterden, Kent. TN30 6EP
Tel: 01580 764225   Fax: 01580 763720   Email: sales@redbooks-maps.co.uk